What Others Are Saying

Sam Ali has hit a home run with Generations and Generations of Wealth. Sam proves that becoming wealthy is not about rocket science—it's about common sense and hard work!

—Rob Wood,
Special Projects Director, HyperGold Web Services

A perfectly structured masterpiece for retirement and wealth building for the entire family. Sam has a passion to pave the road and navigate the middle-class Americans to early retirement like the super rich.

—Marnye Strand,
Account Representative, Fidelity National Title Company

Excellent! Powerful! Thoughtful! Creative! This is Sam's real-life experience in book form. A retirement investment advice to live by. If you want to retire early and be rich, do exactly what Sam instructs in this book.

—Javier M. Chavarria,
Principal, JC Engineering

Wow! Sam Ali's Secrets are the most thought-provoking and powerful guiding light to becoming a millionaire landlord. Build your confidence in retirement and wealth building by emulating his real-life experiences. For example, his generations and generations wealth secret—the principal wealth-building scheme—is sturdy, reliable, and lucrative. Study this book from cover to cover, follow its recommendations, and it will transform your retirement life and also the lives of your loved ones.

—Welch Travel Service

Very instructive and most inspiring retirement-building book. I urge every middle-class American to buy this book.

—Elwood J. Clement,
Enrolled Agent, Clement Tax & Bookkeeping

A retirement financial genius book! This is the author's color of retirement perfection. An all-embracing book to guide you to a total retirement financial freedom. Retiring early and being rich is one of the author's strong assertions. Our advice: Buy it. Read it. Do it. And excel.

—California Housing Co., LLC

Brilliant idea, jam-packed with secrets for comfortable retirement. This book will rediscover and redeem the American retirement dream. Attain the gold standard secret of this most trusted book—you can retire early and be rich.

—Bonn Construction

Fabulous! This book is a jewel to treasure. Sam's passive stream of retirement income is the way to retire. It is truly the complete retirement guide for the day jobber—a must-read book for the middle-class worker interested in creating generations and generations of wealth and in pursuit of happiness.

—Equity Advance Properties, LLC

THE COMPLETE GUIDE TO CREATING
Generations & Generations
OF WEALTH™

THE COMPLETE GUIDE TO CREATING *Generations & Generations* OF WEALTH™

retirement innovation for the middle class

Sam M. Ali

Tate Publishing & *Enterprises*

Published by Tate Publishing & Enterprises, LLC
127 E. Trade Center Terrace | Mustang, Oklahoma 73064 USA
1.888.361.9473 | www.tatepublishing.com

Tate Publishing is committed to excellence in the publishing industry. The company reflects the philosophy established by the founders, based on Psalm 68:11,
"The Lord gave the word and great was the company of those who published it."

Cover design by Amber Gulilat
Interior design by Jeff Fisher

Published in the United States of America

ISBN: 978-1-61566-484-9

1. Business & Economics, Personal Finance, Retirement Planning
2. Business & Economics, Real Estate, Self-Help
09.12.22

Praises and Thanks

All the praises and thanks are to God
for The Complete Guide to Creating
Generations and Generations of Wealth

This is a powerful retirement building plan for creating generations and generations of wealth by investing in duplexes, triplexes, or fourplexes in real estate and ultimately achieving the gold standard secret (chapter one).

I am privileged to be offering my advice during these troubled economic times, which present a challenge to retirement planning. My heart goes out to the middle class (working class) who lost jobs during the economic storm or those who fear they're on the brink of financial ruin. May the wisdom of this guide book find them accelerating their good fortune once more. Nonetheless, know that we are all fortunate to live in one of the most sought after and magnificent places in the world called America. This is the USA—grade A—all the way, where we, Americans, stand steadfast hand-in-hand to weather the storm by sacrifice and innovation. (Try investing in a third-world country, where you will be controlled by the ruler's rules instead of the peoples' rules.) It is my great joy and privilege to be part of America. We should all have pride in our flag, truly an awesome symbol of life, liberty, and the pursuit of happiness. I deeply appreciate and respect those who have built this great country of ours, and I look forward to working with and serving my fellow Americans.

I hope the material in this book will give you confidence in building your own retirement wealth. Not only does it inspire and instruct, but it also gives you some blank spaces to write notes to continually remind yourself of your long-term goals, and it provides purchase and management guidance for your retirement investments. Simply put, I want you to be serious about this motivational, educational, and wealth-building book. As you will soon learn, I am not only an author, but also a doer—a walking proof. Trust me. If you want to catch this retirement train, with tremendous honors, you'd better get down to business and start preparing for your retirement journey based on these time-tested principles. Build your confidence by emulating my true life experiences. I used the tools described in this book to gain daily joy and dream fulfillment. This is also a complete guide to the pursuit of living in harmony with an ever-dynamic, changing world, while following God's rules. While I hope you'll come to appreciate and utilize this book's wisdom and strong advice, rest assured, I have not only set the tone to it but also the criteria for retiring with ease in the way of creating generations and generations of wealth. Now open your mind's eye and begin the journey. May God bless you.

The idea for this work was in my subconscious mind-set for years and notes from my personal diary helped bring it to fruition. I must thank my friends and coworkers at the U. S. Food and Drug Administration (FDA) who assisted me in this great effort. This cherished book will unquestionably help anyone *rediscover* and *redeem* the American retirement dream with stunning success. I'll sincerely thank God for that: Halleluiah, Alham-du-lilla, Boruch Hashem, Jai Bhagwan/Namaste, Salamat Sa Diyos, Alabar a Dios, Gan xie shen/Gum ger suen (Praise the God or praise be to God, or blessed be God).

Thank you so much, folks!
—Sam M. Ali

Dedication

This book is dedicated to my wife and to my daughter.

Their encouragement and support from the very inception of the manuscript stipulation and production to its final publication far exceeded my expectations. I am truly proud of their perseverance in nurturing this book for its merit and importance in our lives as well as the lives of future generations and generations to come.

Acknowledgments

First of all, I would like to thank the publisher, Tate Publishing, for recognizing this as a momentous inspirational and wealth-building book and for meeting the publishing deadline. Thanks to the acquisitions staff, Melissa Huffer and Sara Wood. Special thanks to executive and productions staff, principally Rachael Sweeden and Dave Dolphin. Thank you for your superb effort, editing staff, especially Curtis Winkle, Hannah Tranberg, and Lauren Downen, its reviewing crews, and thanks to cover design staff and illustrations staff, first and foremost to Amber Gulilat and Jeff Fisher. Big thanks to the marketing staff and multimedia staff, particularly Mark Mingle. Again, thanks a bunch to the entire Tate Publishing team for having faith in this arduous and milestone project, as well as for their continuous encouragement and support throughout the process.

A number of my coworkers at the U. S. Food and Drug Administration (FDA) suggested that I write this book after they benefited from my real estate investing advice. Lili Carr and NarNar, especially, inspired me during a luncheon break some years ago.

Many thanks to: Vebina Sethi, Marie Kinkade, Shirley Imura, Warren Savary, Lance DeSouza, Chris Yee, Sergio Chavez,

Norma Rodgers, Marshalette Edwards, Larkin Buckalew, John Liu, Linda Shook, Randy Zielinski, Wayne Jefferson, Charla Tate, Lourdes Trinidad, Terrence Gee, and Jennifer DeGroot for providing invaluable help and assistance early on. Thanks to my photographer, B. Gibson (Bruce) Holcomb, for his professional work on my portrait.

My sincere thanks to Golda Mason, Juan Morales, Lawton Lum, Mei Chiung Huang (Jo), Lealand Lee, Elsa Yu, and Elaine Yip, who researched information on how to thank God in several different languages. Special thanks to Nawied Amin for providing assistance in formatting the manuscript. Thanks to Elgin Williams and Karen Bush, who provided Web site assistance. Thanks a million to Paul Peterson for his review and editorial comments on a draft of this book.

Finally, my heartfelt thanks to my wife, Yasmin, and to my daughter, Mahtab, for their support in embracing this difficult task. My wife and daughter are truly my daily joy, my daily inspirational confidence building, and a source of my purpose-driven inner strength. I love you both dearly.

Above all, I sincerely thank God for blessing my efforts—blessed are those who truly believe in the wisdom and strong advice of this most trusted book and in retiring early and being rich. Halleluiah, Alham-du-lilla, Boruch Hashem, Jai Bhagwan/ Namaste, Salamat Sa Diyos, Alabar a Dios, Gan xie shen/Gum ger suen (Praise the God, or all praise belongs to God, or blessed be God).

Table of Contents

Foreword

This perfectly structured masterpiece is the result of the author's twenty-two years of extensive personal experiences in the making. Sam seriously honors his own beliefs and commitments by sharing his tremendous depth of knowledge and wisdom with the rest of us. He has decided to share his time-tested method in the book form, including inspirational confidence building for retirement innovation, retirement income secrets and the secret to surpassing your current income and retiring early and being rich in creating generations and generations of wealth. This is what the book is all about, and Sam calls it the "most trusted book." As an *inspirational motto*, Sam truthfully believes and reveals the supreme inspirational confidence building and his secret that: *"Cash is king, but cash flow is retirement king."*

One of the main themes is the replacement of the traditional retirement annuity, which has largely disappeared in America and, for now, we are up against the wall. This book deserves a special place among the middle class. He explains that during President Ronald Reagan's

Administration (1981–89), certain members of Congress, aided by corporate lobbyists and special interest groups, changed the principles of the American retirement system. Employer-funded retirement plans, where they still exist, are not as generous as in the past. Sam recommends that we lobby to bring back the old retirement system or at least something better than what we have now. In the meantime, we need to start building our own path toward retirement success. Hence, the value of this book.

Sam thoroughly describes how the average person can create a never-ending passive stream of retirement income by means of a retirement money machine called a small business. He maintains that this is the only bridge over the troubled waters. He believes we Americans are among the best at innovation. He admits that it requires considerable work to create a money-making machine for our golden years, but he implores us to take this golden opportunity to regain a retirement annuity like the previous generation enjoyed, and in so doing create generations and generations of wealth. He cautions us to get the ball rolling now for a predictable financial future or face dire consequences. Sam coined the term "born retired," born with a silver spoon in your mouth, so to speak. He puts in plain words how the children of the super rich, unlike those of the middle class, are "born retired" from the usual day-job obligations. He sees one fundamental difference between the super rich and the middle class; the super rich provide their inheritance wealth up front, whereas the middle class give up their inheritance wealth when they pass away.

Once your small business starts growing with cash flow, you will be on your way to exiting your day job and entering early retirement. You are then fully qualified, graduated, and you may drum up the small business to, as Sam calls it, the advanced stage of retirement. Kudos to Sam. He gets an A+ for sharing his secrets. Thank you so much, Sam.

—Yasmin Ali, RN, BSN
Author's first associate

Introduction

The principal source of my revenue for retirement is a passive stream of retirement income (PSORI), derived from owning rental properties. This is the basis for the creation of generations and generations of wealth, and it is truly my elegant retirement heritage. PSORI is a prerequisite for gaining access to the single most prestigious governing criterion: *cash flow.* Cash flow is the one sign of hope in overcoming retirement financial woe. Our cash flow can provide a steady retirement income for the middle class reminiscent of what the super rich enjoy. This entire process is attested by my more than two decades of personal experience in the field. We need to plant the seeds of this work of art in our loved ones and their loved ones too. Tell them the truth, that things are not easy these days. They may have to stay longer with papa and mama in weathering out tough economic conditions and contemplate on challenges.

Our retirement system has changed. What's changed? A lot of things. This comes at a time when we are facing a host of demands by the next wave of retirees, who need to pay increasing medical, energy, food, and other essential costs. I am afraid we are going to see more dreadful things happen in our golden years if we do not get our act together soon. However, this book will help. Given the magnitude of the retirement problem, let's not play the blaming game anymore. We will innovate and change to be better than ever before. Have confidence in this American icon for its breakthrough approaches, for creating much-needed wealth for the new wave of retirees. Life's needs are getting sophisticated and dynamic, so let's catch the moving train and innovate and lay the end of the line to our destination (our golden years). Operating a real estate small business is the answer to a very successful retirement. The key is rental ownership. And this book is the key for that guidance. If you pay strict attention to my guiding principles and carefully apply them, you will be financially equipped, as well as philosophically, psychologically, physically, and spiritually equipped, to prosper now and in your retirement years. And this will set the stage for success for your descendants and their heirs as well. Like me, I expect you, my associate, to inspire others.

The book covers the following topics:

1. Building wealth as the super rich do (Creating generations and generations of wealth.)
2. Motivating by means of inspirational confidence building.
3. Developing a passive stream of retirement income for life (PSORI).
4. Eliminating the risk associated with the acquisition of duplexes, triplexes, or fourplexes (small business).
5. Using down payment from your 401(k) or 403(b) retirement or thrift savings plan (TSP) federal government retirement plan, or best yet, derived from personal savings, and/or borrowing a portion from a rich uncle to purchase a duplex, triplex, or a fourplex.

6. Achieving the gold standard and the gold standard secret of this book.
7. Managing with the best property management tools.
8. Overcoming investment fears.
9. Creating wealth for loved ones.
10. Being organized in life.
11. Being conscious of God in your daily life through piety and alms.
12. Enjoying the responsibility and life.

Through this book's wisdom, we will see the world in a new way, just as the super rich see it. How? Well, the complicated answer is the super rich do not complain that their gas, electric, water bills are too high, that their TV bill is too high, that their grocery bill is too high, and so on and so forth since these are basic necessities of living. We cannot continue living without some of them. Then why in the world should I waste my precious, precious time in discussing such things? It blows my mind that the middle class dwell on these issues day in and day out. We'll let others provide these services for us knowing it is just a small fraction of our revenue. What the super rich "complain" about is their next investment strategy to acquire another retirement business or how to drum up the retirement business to the next level. For us, this would be a duplex or a triplex or a fourplex and then working toward attaining the gold standard secret (chapter one) of this true-to-life book or straightforwardly moving up the small business to the advanced stage of retirement (chapter ten). In reality, the whole conversation, for the middle class, should be based on learning how to bring in more money to our bank account, or for that matter, to our reserve (emergency cash cushion supply) bank account.

The super rich will help each other or at least bat around some ideas or deals they made, which they keep under wraps. The idea here is to change your subconscious mind-set (chapter seven) and start thinking and acting like the super rich, earn a lot of money, and eventually you will come to regard the basic living expenses as peanuts. Did you appreciate and recognize the value of this message? Please do not go to the next family dinner table and try to change the mood or subconscious mind-sets of others. Remember, having a little knowledge of this innovation is a perilous journey. First, you have to learn the basic concepts in this educational conscious mind-set book and then apply them. Purchase just a duplex, triplex, or a fourplex to start with and then, turn the property into a money-making machine by the passive stream of retirement income (chapter two), which is the top secret ingredient of the recipe. After accomplishing that mission, then it is time to change the mood or subconscious mind-sets of others. Of course, creating the great big one is achieving the gold standard secret of your retirement innovation, thereby creating generations and generations of wealth. And please also do not go around to other people's dinner table parties and discuss it. Others may think you are irrational, so please keep it a secret until you have actually accomplished your goals and then spread the good word (wisdom) of being well-to-do with style. But for now, please read and highlight facts or motivational phrases that excite you, inspire you, flag them with post-its, work on it, read and re-read if necessary, study it, picture it in your mind's eye—*that's the learn-by-heart secret* to remembering the book's main points. Of course, this would give you the stamina, encouragement, and prepare you to apply its lessons. And this learning process should be our fruit-bearing ambitious journey. So, folks, let's hit the book.

Please be knowledgeable about real-estate ownership, which is the ultimate toolkit for a massive sustained success if you are willing to learn from this great effort. Please adore this masterwork for it will guide you to obtaining much-needed retirement wealth in your golden years. Some of my daily compelling force of inspirational confidence building is my collection of words of inspiration for innovation found at the end of every chapter. These are taken from my diary, entitled *Golden Rules and Best Advice for*

Retirement Investments in Real Estate. I'm inspired and excited. I say, reveal and show your real passion for wealth accumulation via this book's wisdom. This is our moment and our time. A rolled out red carpet has been placed before you. The golden opportunity is knocking at the door. Please open the door and walk on the red carpet to your chosen retirement destiny.

Author's Appreciation

I want to congratulate you and express my gratitude and appreciation for taking time to read this inspirational and instructional book. Please be aware that I have a deep passion for sharing my retirement income building system with you. The time you spend reading this book coupled with taking action will produce stunning results because, after all, I have time-tested it. The book is filled with the wisdom and strong advice of passive stream of retirement income (PSORI) for creating generations and generations of wealth for you and your loved ones. And please, don't be late in realizing that one doesn't get rich by working at a day job.

This book is not only a guide to creating generations and generations of wealth but also is the nucleus of complete practical wisdom for living in pursuit of happiness. It's a mini workbook too, helping you cope with a prolonged transformation. I urge you to write down some of your goals and visions. Be inspired to take action. You'll need to make it happen in having a successful retirement journey. You purchased this true-to-life book with your hard-earned money. Trust me; my advice will repay you exponentially. No false promises. This is truly your specialist in guiding your retirement and succession planning. You have chosen the best of the best. Now that you are the owner of this masterpiece, be serious, be happy, be a real go-getter, and make it happen. Are you with me? Allow your brain to absorb the wisdom and graduate with honors. Happy reading and retirement planning!

Please reiterate in your own handwriting in the space below:

I will transform my present retirement building plan into a small business through the wisdom of this book. I will retire early from my day job, and, in doing so, I will create generations and generations of wealth for myself and my loved ones.

Your Signature

Today's Date

Great! Good job!

Chapter 1

Creating Generations and Generations of Wealth
The Gold Standard

RETIREMENT INNOVATION

Inspirational confidence building is the key to the business of retirement innovation. Retirement innovation is getting creative out of necessity and is an important element of reclaiming lasting prosperity in the golden years. A basic Americanism principle has been echoed time and again by President Barack Obama: "Innovation has been essential to our prosperity in the past, and it will be essential to our prosperity in the future." The wisdom of this book provides the complete guide to this retirement innovation—retiring early and being rich. In fact, it is the complete crash course for the business of retirement innvation. It is uniquely different from any other type of retirement investment course. So get ready to retire early from your day job and experience true excellence. Please realize the time-tested ultimate retirement innovation. Expect the best of the best from the best and the brightest system of doing—the plutocrat way—the super rich way. This innovation will make a splash for middle-class America. It is the obvious choice. Americans are excellent innovators. A time for change is in the air. Change and innovation are the essence of living. It is a very opportune idea of change and optimism. A change we can believe in and experience. A change we can trust. This masterpiece book will bring about the most desired change in our retirement journey. Of course, change brings anxiety. Change is more pronounced today than at any other time in the past. Apparently, even our climate is changing and the earth is in peril. We cannot be left to drift and be caught completely off guard in our golden years. Therefore, we have to change our way of living too. I can say confidently, now is the time to put a stake in the ground and open the door for a record-breaking retirement lifestyle. Sometimes you can have it all.

It is time to rethink about the words *retirement* and *wealth*. For better or worse, the American retirement systems have changed. I believe they have changed forever, to the detriment of many. We are sailing on a leaking retirement ship that is on the verge of sinking. It is an American revolution. There is no turning back. Due to staggering and ever-inflating living expenses, it is getting harder and harder to retire comfortably. Neither the federal government nor corporate America wants to generously contribute to our retirement. It seems as though nobody really wants to finance our golden years. What can we do?

During the President Ronald Reagan Administration (1981–89), new laws were enacted that affected the retirement benefits for many workers. Introduced for federal civil service employees was the thrift savings plan (TSP), federal retirement thrift investment board, and in the private sector it was the 401(k) or 403(b) retirement plan. (The old retirement system gave the employee a just and fair compensation for his/her thirty or more years of service by means of a monthly retirement annuity check for life.) New government retirement mandates favored corporate America and resulted in granting employee retirement benefit to a minimal. I believe some wise lobbyists and special interest groups working on Capitol Hill were largely behind this legislation. Capitalism has created more corporate millionaires and billionaires in the early twenty-first century than any past century. Nowadays, greed appears to be an intrinsic aspect of capitalism. We hear time and again "get the rascals out of Congress" or "stop the rhetoric and do your job, Congress." It is becoming increasingly clear that whoever runs and wins the race makes the rules in favor of the super rich while denying privileges for the poor and middle classes. Once Congresspersons are seated on Capitol Hill, they frequently forget the dilemmas of the middle class and the poor. Congress appears to be overly influenced by corporate lobbyists and special interest groups. Our elected representatives should know better. They need to represent everyone equally and not favor themselves or special interest groups. They ought to clearly understand that our government is "government of the people, by the people, for the people"—President Abraham Lincoln's words. It's the moment in time to demand fairness, dignity, and respect for middle-class America.

On a brighter side, we will avoid the pitfalls and blunders by taking this golden opportunity to innovate and strike gold in crafting a far better system and still attain our retirement dream akin to the American dream. This is the golden opportunity to ensure you put your best foot forward and get on board for a retirement annuity check like the previous generation enjoyed. We will, in fact, be creating generations and generations of wealth by doing so. We have a profound obligation to rescue our retirement benefits once and for all. It is a once in a lifetime golden opportunity. Let's take decisive action and hit the ground running. Let's be certain of where we are going. Let our dreams come true. Perhaps, for some, it is more than a dream; it's the American dream.

"I have a dream!" One of the most notable speeches in American history by Martin Luther King, Jr., which prompted the Civil Rights Act in 1964. He further said, "Let freedom ring from the curvaceous slopes of California." This masterwork is born in California and made in the USA. Incidentally, this author has a dream too.

- I have a dream that one day we, the American middle class, will rise up through the wisdom and strong advice of this book and earn like the super rich.
- I have a dream that one day we, the American middle class, will retire like the super rich.
- I have a dream that one day we, the American middle-class, including my daughter, will one day live by creating generations and generations of wealth like the super rich.

My dream is on its way to reality. I may be one of the first to embrace this golden opportunity to invest in myself and apply its principles in real time to create an elegant retirement heritage. Keep in mind, we Americans are among the best innovators. Let's innovate to a retirement money machine generator called a business, a small business in correct perspective, and take home a passive stream of retirement income (PSORI). For me, this is the only bridge over troubled waters. Unlike others, I want to be both an innovator and inspirational leader. It is the retirement freedom I deserve. In fact, freedom is the bedrock for our successes in this country. Therefore, unleash the energy of retirement freedom. I vow to be proactive in developing success in everything, especially in retirement financial freedom.

Confidently, with our self-reliance and accountability, we will slowly and surely march to retirement success. Now we can actually start to invest in ourselves as the super rich do and use this powerful force to generate generations and generations of wealth for us middle-class Americans. I have seen some super-rich individuals become victims of their own wealth and success. Some are unprepared to receive colossal wealth and fame. They have lavish and conspicuous lifestyles. For some, wealth appears to be crippling. They are doomed to be escorted by security guards wherever they go. I certainly don't want that for myself. For me, too much of anything is not good. Moderation in all things. We will cherish the wealth as the super rich do but in a more controlled way. Let's take a serious glimpse of their wealth power while extracting some positive features of their lifestyle and buying frenzy. We can enjoy both worlds, knowing we are in control of our financial destiny. The question is, shouldn't we be willing to sacrifice a little to create generations and generations of wealth? I guarantee it; otherwise I would not be where I am. Here, the key to success is by way of innovation, starting from a strong foundation. Prosperity thinking is the key ingredient of success. Sustained success only comes to those who are truly success conscious. Again, the key element is retirement innovation. I am honored to be one of the messengers for this innovation. Be happy! Be inspired! Who does not want a miracle in retirement? In principle, this enduring masterpiece is prospecting for major accomplishments in our retirement life and beyond. It is a brilliant and majestic blockbuster wealth-creating idea to become rich and remain rich. So get inspired!

Folks, this is not a philosophy book. This is the book's wisdom and strong advice to thrive to retirement success. We Americans will stand steadfast and anchor our core values and innovate to an investment scheme for our retirement. Remember, you are reading from my secret diary, my way of life. Please transform yourself by doing what I advocate. It is an intriguing approach used by the best and the brightest. It is not a whole new chapter in history; it is the super riches' time-honored retirement method.

So, keep your morale up. Go for it. But wait! Just a bit longer. First you have to graduate by absorbing the wisdom of my time-tested device. Please understand that most people become rich by owning a business, not by working at a day job. However, a day job may have been the prerequisite to business ownership. Know the facts of this business first. Having little knowledge of this retirement innovation is a precarious generalization because there are no makeups for mishaps. You just can't afford to make many mistakes, by any means, even in the process of getting hold of cash flow machine for life. Learn the facts and make the educated move. I believe that this book's grand message is built on a strong reputation for retirement income stability and reliability. I took advantage of this golden opportunity to make sure I was on track for a rewarding retirement life. Never underestimate the power of this retirement innovation—it is time tested proven. Patience, diligence, and a systematic approach work best for this innovation. Rest assured, this retirement plan will set us apart from other retirement plans because we will be creating generations and generations of wealth.

Creating Generations and Generations of Retirement Wealth

It is my perfectly structured masterpiece, for it is my mark of excellence and also an enduring commitment to excellence. I prefer to not apply an acronym for the title of this book: Generations and Generations of Wealth (GGW or GGOW or GAGOW), because I personally love to say the full phrase: generations and generations of wealth. Don't you? My associate? While it enthusiastically inspires me to verbalize the repeat of words generations-generations attached to word wealth, it serves as: promising, comforting, strengthening, longing, and as an ultimate passion of wealth ownership with a touch of elegance and spicy-hot inspirational confidence building, therefore, the title of the book—generations and generations of wealth. The title shines admirably and fosters eagerness and readiness to fulfilling its core mission of creating generations and generations of wealth. This extraordinary (book) title has the power to cook up and invent challenges and ultimate triumphs, which are embedded in it—if you articulate it slowly with a deep sense of feeling. It encourages the joy of wealth creation or simply enjoying it if you have already acquired one of these money machines. A thing of beauty is a joy forever, and this is precisely the intent of the title. This is what I call *top-notch inspirational title secret.* It's a lifeline and a lifetime motivator and, undeniably, this title has the well-heeled effective tip for inspiration of wealth creation.

One of the true joys in my life is, of course, to earn my own retirement income through a business entrepreneurship and by doing something I am enormously passionate about and by making a real contribution to the lives of my loved ones too. My blueprint is quite robust and its major exercise is to run a tight ship and be known for being a small business leader for inspirational and procedural guidance.

This blueprint gives me a sense of purpose, a sense of security, a sense of happiness, a sense of success, a sense of contentment, and it certainly hails in me the purpose-driven virtue: Pearls of retirement wisdom and strong advice to teach others to understand the retirement dilemma we are facing and its clear solution. For this innovation, there is a one-size-fits-all. We will also win the seal of approval from our loved ones. Winning in life is necessary; it is the survival of the fittest. And, sure enough, the silver lining in all of this is that we actually begin to *rediscover* and *redeem* the American dream of ownership and self-control of our retirement and wealth. This is great!

Moreover, if your business plan spirals into the next stage of retirement, you will be well on your way to exiting your day job for an early retirement, and you may move to the advanced stage of retirement. This gives me the unique opportunity to continually thank the provider, the cherisher, the almighty God. Thank you,

God, for uplifting our spirit to a worldly gain for financial freedom: Halleluiah, Alham-du-lilla, Boruch Hashem, Jai Bhagwan/ Namaste, Salamat Sa Diyos, Alabar a Dios, Gan xie shen/Gum ger suen (Praise the God, or all praise belongs to God, or blessed be God).

Achieving the Gold Standard and Gold Standard Secret

In God we trust. I believe in God, the Supreme Being who is the ruler of the universe, the provider, the cherisher, the sustainer, the almighty, you name it. His is the universe. I believe that we are a purpose-driven people. The point here is that God created this world for a purpose and each of us was created by him for a purpose. Therefore, it is from a deep sense of purpose that I sincerely believe in teaching others what God certified me to deliver. I have made mistakes in real-estate acquisitions, and God has time and again corrected, perfected, and certified me. Yes, I took some missteps but not many. Hopefully you will not repeat them. Believe me; you are receiving a foolproof education. Learn from my struggles. If we all truly listen to the voices of this inspirational and instructional book and do what it recommends, there is no one blocking our move up except ourselves.

To me, the message is profoundly clear: to deliver secret messages to anyone willing to listen. To teach and guide others to create generations and generations of wealth by investing in either a duplex, a triplex, or a fourplex piece of real estate. A duplex, a triplex, or a fourplex is a small business. For me, owning a fourplex is the gold standard of retirement innovation investment. A lesser gold standard is a duplex or triplex. I explain in detail why the virtues of owning a fourplex constitutes the gold standard. To receive more bang for your buck, use some of your present retirement funds, or best yet, derived from personal savings, and/or borrowing a portion from a rich uncle to first acquire a fourplex. To fast-track this project, hang in there, keep your day job, and let your tenants help pay off the mortgage obligation until finally you possess a free-and-clear title. A free-and-clear title is almost like owning a bank and embracing it. Having a free-and-clear title is what I call the—*gold standard secret*—of our retirement innovation. Just imagine the feeling of being debt free. This is one of the climax secrets of this book. The season for continuous beauty lies on the footsteps of your money machine if you have a gold standard secret in your hand. This gold standard secret will re-invent your annuity check, restore your trust and self-confidence for a reliable passive stream of retirement income (PSORI). Similarly, the lesser gold standard—a duplex or triplex—can also attain the gold standard secret of our money-making machine bank that grants money without incurring bank interest charges. And the best part is, it's yours for life.

The key to big results is having no mortgage payments, and this will immensely reassure and strengthen our foothold. Likewise, I have used the cash flow from increasing rents—fair market rents—to pay off mortgage debt faster. For some of us, this may take seven to fifteen (having a fifteen-year loan) years to accomplish, while others may require more or less time to attain the gold standard secret. The essential elements here are gradual reduction in loan balance paid from cash flow and whatever additional (above and beyond mortgage payments) you can afford to make each month. This will accelerate your retirement reward. Our win will come at a price but think of that earning—PSORI—a far-reaching gold cup reward. How great! And rewarding! We certainly have something grand to work toward and something grand to wait for. Make no mistake. After obtaining a free-and-clear title, in due course, you may be early retirement ready. You could even retire from your day job by way of cash flow streaming from the receipt of monthly passive stream of retirement income (PSORI). Moreover, rest assured, I have validated the PSORI line approach.

The hurdle that I crossed in acquiring my first small business was well worth the effort. When I drive by at one of my properties, I say to myself, "These properties are ours and will give generations and generations of wealth to us and to our descendants." I believe that these are reflections of God's blessings on us for sustained success. To me, my properties are my bank, my money-making machines for life in creating generations and generations of wealth. For some folks, owning just one such retirement machine (small business) would do the job. The defining characteristic of the real estate retirement investment is that it provides a passive stream of retirement income (PSORI) for life. The harder I worked, the better the result. With a clear conscious mind-set, I learned that the process of working hard takes courage and patience, and double the reward is there for those who work hard. Whether you plan to repeat the process by purchasing another property is entirely up to you. Nevertheless, an ambitious and milestone project with a clear pathway has already been carved for you, my associate.

Summary of requirements for achieving the gold standard secret:

- Use some of your present retirement fund or, best yet, derived from personal savings, and/or borrowing a portion from a rich uncle to purchase a fourplex (gold standard).
- While keeping your day job, you (using some portion of take-home pay) and your tenants (rental income) will pay off the mortgage, and you will obtain a free-and-clear title (gold standard secret).
- After obtaining a free-and-clear title, net operating retirement income (NORI) will now equal cash flow (CF), chapter four, allowing you to retire early from your day job and/or move to the advanced stage of retirement.

Progressive and Regressive Tax Theory

After graduating from this life-changing book and attaining the gold standard secret, you'll be avoiding the earning style of middle class. In fact, you'll be earning a *passive activity income* (chapter two). The middle class are also called the tax-paying class, or the working class, or even the lower class. Let us elevate ourselves to some level below the super rich. Go ahead and ask me at this point, "What do the super rich do?" "What is their strategic plan of action?" The super rich have a master plan, and one of the fundamentals is not giving much of their wealth to the IRS. The IRS puts up with the super rich because the tax laws favor the super rich and are geared to having the middle class pay more than their fair share. Part of the super rich landscape is to pay as little tax as possible. The middle class are "informed" that the tax laws are progressive (pay more as you earn more) when, in fact, they are regressive (pay less as you earn more or pay as little tax as possible if you are a member of the super rich dynasty owning a business). Ours is a small business, and it holds to the same doctrine. The point is that the super rich always get away from paying their fair share. They get their retirement money in a passive way. Their income goes into a cash register and is banked, the profits offset by claiming deductions and credits for business expenses. The business *profit and loss statement* may show a loss, yet the business actually thrives and makes money. It's so agonizing that the middle class have to go through extraneous squabble to claim their fair share of taxes.

Being a middle-class day jobber, the IRS takes one-third income tax withholdings off the top of your paycheck without your permission. The agency is so powerful that it can take your home if you do not pay your taxes or put you behind bars. Again, the super rich get away from paying their fair share of taxes by claiming business operating expenses. Business is their way of life. It's true, the super rich *also* prevent the IRS from taking their home by forming a business entity called *Inc.* (Incorporated) or an *LLC* (Limited Liability Company), so on and so forth.

In conclusion, the super rich exert their domination of wealth ownership and prosperity by all feasible means. Folks, we have to move away from this IRS-middle class struggle forever. The raging answer to this treatment by IRS is, undeniably, the small business, and our skill-set shines and is in line with the super rich system.

Pay No Upfront Income Taxes to the IRS

We'll endeavor to be better than the super rich by pursuing a balanced lifestyle. Conversely, the secret message here is to turn things around by merely owning a small business called a duplex, or a triplex, or a fourplex, and then I am just like a super rich person. I virtually pay no upfront income taxes to the IRS. For example, owning a fourplex, I collect monthly rents: passive stream of retirement income (PSORI) totaling $4,000, in my example, each of the four tenants pays $1,000 rent ($1,000 x 4 = $4,000/mo) and the total for the year equals $48,000 ($4,000 x 12 = $48,000/yr). You see, each month I collect a total of $4,000 in my hand, right. What's the big deal, right? But where is the IRS? I immediately take $4,000 to my bank, and at the end of the year I have deposited a sum of $48,000 in my bank account. Wow! This is remarkable, unforgivable. This is what I call the *business bank deposit secret,* and it is truly changing my lifestyle forever. Do you see the clear difference between day job income verses business revenue (super rich way of earning revenue)?

Since fair market rents are the same in any given region, the attractiveness of retirement investment in real estate is that a small investor like me will earn the exact same percentage of investment return as big legendary investors—the super rich. To me, this is super rich's full plate of same percent hospitality investment return for us. This is what I call the *same-percentage return secret.* This is a big, big plus in my retirement investment with a smooth path (same percentage of return), no bumpy ride. Truly, ownership of real estate has great retirement rewards for me and my loved ones. Remember, I am rich but not super rich. However, I have the super rich's secret retirement money machine. I do not pay upfront income taxes. By just owing a piece of real estate and renting it, I have a legal business, a small business. In almost all cities, no business license is required. Again, the federal tax policy favors the super rich. If it were in my control, I'd never ever work for someone else and I'd let the IRS coffers run dry. Don't get me wrong. I do pay income taxes at the end of the year. But I will be claiming all the legitimate associated operating expenses (OE), including property taxes, mortgage interest, depreciation expenses, maintenance expenses, improvements (if any), and so on and so forth, and in the process owe very little taxes. Not weekly, not monthly, but a little yearly. That's what the super rich do! This is what I call *business income tax secret.*

Please, pause reading here and consider the point. Mind you, this is powerful stuff.

____

____

____

Get inspired. Please seriously heed and unveil your true passion for wealth accumulation and write your thoughts here:

____

____

____

Did you say, "I want to be rich? I want to be rich too!" Oh, well. Very well, then that's what we'll do.

Possession Transfer Dilemmas

The tax agencies want citizens to remain in the middle class so that they can collect more revenue. Get the drift? So we will follow the guiding example set by the super rich, even on our death beds. We will create an entity as the super rich do to accomplish just that. How? By creating a *trust* (chapter seven). Some specialized tax planning may be necessary, depending on your present or anticipated future net worth. Beyond taxes, my estate plan should take other objectives into account. If I were to die tomorrow, what legacy would I leave? I should periodically re-examine my revocable living trusts to see if they conform to my objectives. Also, I'll look at the beneficiary listings on my retirement plans to see if they're still appropriate.

Act Like a Super-Rich Person

I feel rich whenever I go on vacation to the Fiji Islands, Hawaii, Puerto Rico, Dubai, Canada, London or buy gifts and souvenirs, and so on and so forth because I know my tenants will help to foot the bill with their rent checks. And I know my spending limit. This keeps my blood pressure normal, like a gift from God to proceed with his favor. What feeling could be better than this? Act like a super rich person while being a modestly wealthy person and being a step above the member of the middle class, and the American dream will come true from beginning to end (generations to generations). Again, what feeling could be better than this?

Prenuptial Agreement Dilemmas

What does the average middle-class person know about the ramification of a prenuptial agreement? Do we even care about it? Remember, one of the themes of this book is to create generations and generations of wealth and pass it through the inheritance pipeline on to our loved ones. Once we obtain wealth, we will want to preserve it for ourselves and for our descendants. We should require our loved ones to enter into a prenuptial agreement before getting married. This is how the super rich do it, and so should we. The underlying principle is to keep wealth in the family and guard against possible misuse. Consider family wealth as a hard-earned prized treasure, a power-dynasty, and be fully cognizant of its intrinsic power, which has the ability to help us in keeping our family in sound prosperity and flourishing for many years to come. This is what I call the *everlasting prosperity secret.* So, to follow this path correctly, it is important to have a prenuptial agreement signed in advance. This should be openly discussed between the bride and groom. It is understandable that there may be some resistance from a marriage partner who does not already possess wealth. One way to enlighten a partner is to be frank and explain things in layman terms, stressing the fact that you, as a couple, will want the same for your children. Again, this is basically to protect inherited wealth so that it can be passed on, not squandered.

Pearls of Retirement Wisdom and Strong Advice

I assume this book will not be read by many from the super rich group, but it will certainly unleash the pearls of retirement wisdom and strong advice in the rest of us and in beefing up our new lifestyles. At the very least, it will reveal and elevate us above the middle class beyond belief. I am truly delighted and excited, with great pleasure, to unveil my stored energy *pearls of retirement wisdom* secret message, i.e., to disclose to you, my associate, that the prospect of having my dream come true was, in reality, daunting, especially taking money out of my retirement account and launching into speculative venture. What? Why from my present petty retirement account? Scary stuff! This would give a cold shoulder and a nippy feeling to a middle class especially if I were not following my parents' footsteps to secure my retirement financial future including my loved ones. But my gut feeling was strong, and I had done my homework. My homework involved months of research truly surpassing my expectations. Clearly, it surfaced with nifty—and often thrilling—domino effects! To jump-start my small business, I had to use a chunk of fund from my retirement account. I was excited to take the leap—my gut feeling of owning real estate as a retirement device appeared strong and looked to be the only way to creating a retirement income stream—the super rich way, the IRS-mandated way. At that moment something else prompted that was mind-blowing with even stronger vibes by having the thought of wealth creation for my loved ones. I said, "This is it!" One generation represents me, and the other generation represents my daughter and my grandchildren. Hence, the *generations and generations of wealth* (book) phrase was coined. While it's true I raided my government retirement account, given the research I did, today I am very confident and realized that this resource had a dramatic upward career trajectory, and the gleaming new retirement income stream was my reward. I am firmly convinced that I took the right approach with a down payment of 20 to 40 percent. It's true. I got what I paid for and excelled. I gained access to my PSORI for which I am grateful and extremely proud, and its progress to the advanced stage of retirement is exciting and an effective system. In reality, the outlays buy a mighty retirement machine that lays the golden eggs for our prosperity. My associate may follow suit.

I ask myself:

What could be better than this?

How do I do it?

Where do I start?

You did exactly what your gut instinct said by purchasing this truthful book. Good job and good workable luck to you and your loved ones. To me, it is a retirement treasure, a diamond in the rough, for my prosperity and inspiration. It will take years to accomplish this life-long task, but be ready to receive it on a golden platter for saying, "I deserve this." Remember, you will collect your reward for being patient and doing it.

The next few chapters will guide us to achieving this by owning a duplex, a triplex, or a fourplex real estate and thus preserving the wealth for generations and generations to come.

Why duplex?

Why triplex?

Why fourplex real estate?

Where do I get my down payment for the purchase?

How do I manage my property to riches?

How much wealth is enough wealth?

These questions are central to the theme of this book, and

I'll share my experiences in answering them in a variety of ways, covering this method with proven facts.

I enjoy reading motivational books. To that end, I have collected words of inspirational confidence building for innovation at the end of each chapter. I need that compelling force of confidence for pursuing and doing it. For us middle class, the mainstream income in the form of cash comes from our day job salary. Whereas, income for the super rich is extraordinarily derived from *cash flow* channeling from business enterprise—a river flowing with separate channels of "milk and honey." Its presence indicates a continuous fund from a fail-safe wealth source. Although I'm following the road to riches in a moderate way, I still need the secret passageway to the treasure chest established by the super rich. Of course, we will follow the path of least resistance. So I crafted a similar passageway toward reaching the *cash flow* treasure chest, through inspirational confidence building. This is what I call the *cash is king but cash flow is retirement king secret.* It's a stri*king* success. Great treasure! Triumph for the middle class! This evidently emerges as a timeless motto in support of our retirement innovation for the middle class. Envision where you want to be in seven to fifteen years from now. I say, a gorgeous fourplex with a hefty cash flow befitting a middle class retirement king (or queen). One of my other daily inspirational confidence buildings is tied to a very compelling and controlling inspirational quotation:

> "Best revenge in life is massive success."
>
> —Frank Sinatra

My Massive Success Way of Life:

Success in creating generations and generations of wealth

Success in creating wealth like the super rich (owning a small business)

Success in having a good retirement plan: cash flow and cash savings

Success in having a good estate plan: creating a trust (living trust)

Success in having a good financial plan: self and family, including loved ones

Success in managing time: work, vacation, family, self

Success in working as if everything depended upon me

Success in having a good health plan: including exercise, relaxation, sleep

Success in having warm family relationships: supportive, honest, helping

Success in being a good, loving human being

Success in seeking God's divine approval through heartfelt prayers

Success in seeking peace and happiness via patience and prayers

Success in performing prayers for forgiveness and prayers of thankfulness

Success in fulfilling all my obligations

Success in giving alms to the poor

Success in achieving the best in this world and the next world

This one is one of my major, major directives. I heavily focus on having my best revenge by having massive success in all areas of my life, including:

(1) Financial

(2) Philosophical

(3) Psychological

(4) Physical

(5) Spiritual

I enjoy a balanced lifestyle. I truly believe number one (financial) is the entrance to the rest. This is the controlling standard that produces profound separation, and is greatly underappreciated and inappropriately treasured by the middle class. Financial triumph is one of the special prerogatives of the super rich that give them special status in our society. In fact, this is what actually separates the middle class from the super rich. We middle-class citizens keep our nose to the grindstone and work, and work, for thirty to forty-five years for the m-o-n-e-y, and we devote very little time to numbers two through numbers five, especially number five. Certainly, all these things come to us not without substantial performance expectations. I hope I am terribly wrong in saying that some of us will never be able to afford to retire from our day jobs. It is a big, big dilemma, but thanks to this inspirational and instructional book, you will get efficient and effective retirement answers. I endeavored to put together all the necessary tools that I use to advance my goals and for you to clearly contemplate.

Time to Perfect Yourself as the Author's Associate

Be my associate. I believe that with change comes unique opportunity. In this case, a golden opportunity for you, my associate. The reader will be considered an associate of the author once he/she has graduated, demonstrating a thorough understanding of the wisdom of this book. Realizing that we all are in the same boat, we should all make preparations to take on the challenge together. I know it is a tough call, but come on, please don't be wishy-washy about your retirement. Be the first to experience retirement treasure without limits, since experience is a superb teacher. It is a lifestyle that you will create. Its secrets are well focused. They are written in the hopes that anyone reading, seriously heeding and doing it will retire early and being rich with a good retirement income that is incessant. It is just sheer learning from my way of gaining inspirational confidence building toward wealth and by putting my failures behind. It is through failures that I have perfected myself, using lessons learned from failures to my advantage and moving on. To be completely honest, I feel a need to express and explain in detail this time-tested skill set with inspirational confidence building to everyone (myself included), and especially my associate, who has the patience to learn. It cannot be overstated: patience, patience, patience is the strategic point to planning for your retirement and creating generations and generations of wealth. Gaining resilience by power of patience is the key. To me, the power of patience is *refueling and/or reenergizing*—a renewable phase. My associate should know that many real-estate scholars have placed undue emphasis on the importance of—location, location, location—of the property. I believe it should be more correctly viewed as location, location, *time.* I learned that location is great, but time is a major controlling factor. You know, for example, that in time you can attain the gold standard secret.

Inspirational Confidence Building

"A good title is the title of a successful book."

—Raymond Chandler

"Best revenge in life is massive success."

—Frank Sinatra

"Happiness lies in the joy of achievement and the thrill of creative effort."

—Franklin D. Roosevelt

"You can't just sit there and wait for people to give you that golden dream. You've got to get out there and make it happen for yourself."

—Diana Ross

"Change will not come if we wait for some other person or some other time. We are the ones we've been waiting for. We are the change that we seek."

—President Barack Obama

Chapter 2

Principles of Retirement Concept

RETIREMENT AS A DEFINITION

Government has redefined the principles of the retirement system for the middle class in America. A general definition that most of us understood, or thought we believed by observing our grandparents and/or our parents retire from their day jobs, would include the following desired elements or retirement expectations:

- A pension, either a lump-sum payment or monthly annuity check
- A paid-off mortgage on a primary residence
- Adequate savings and possibly a second home as a retirement investment
- Adequate insurance coverage (medical and life) that is wholly or at least partly subsidized by the former employer
- Time to travel and see new places
- Time to spend with loved ones
- Time to get closer to God
- Time to relax, reflect, entertain, and enjoy hobbies

Sadly, in the present day, some of the above elements or retirement expectations that were previously associated with the dazzling word *retirement* are disappearing.

The old retirement definition ran something like this:

> According to conventional wisdom, *retirement* is the final point of employment where an employee withdraws from the active work force. The employer would provide an annuity (or lump-sum disbursement) to the employee for life after a minimum age and years of service requirements were met, or in the event of a work-related injury or medical condition, provide partial wages in the form of a disability compensation package.

For Social Security, sixty-five is still regarded as the usual age for retirement, although it is gradually increasing to age sixty-seven and higher. Age sixty-two is the earliest retirement age that one can file for reduced benefits. We hear that the Social Security system is running on a thin margin and is heading for a shortage of funds for future generations. However, my associates can retire early from their day job at any age, provided they have adequate cash flow and accumulated wealth.

Passive Stream of Retirement Income (PSORI) and the Super Rich

What is passive stream of retirement income (PSORI)?

Passive stream of retirement income (PSORI, pronounced as P-SO-RI) is a source of revenue for retirement derived from owning rental properties with adequate cash flows. PSORI is our golden eggs. (Realtors call it passive stream of rental income or passive stream of income, or simply, rental income.) It is the way the super rich receive their retirement revenue by a passive source but the most direct way. I collect my retirement rental income each month directly from my tenants, and the taxes on it are not due until the end of the tax year. When I prepare my tax return against it, I claim all operating expenses (OE) as legitimate deductions. This is the passive road to wealth that the super rich use every day, every week, every month, and every year to sustain their super-rich status. Basically, the super rich get richer by cash flow from a business entity. We middle-class retirement investors can do the same thing by simply owning and renting a fourplex, a triplex, or a duplex. Again, investing in a fourplex, a triplex, or a duplex is a type of small business. Cash flow is the secret to retirement success, and it can certainly show us a pathway toward early retirement. To "go with the flow" is considered mediocre. I say, "Go with the cash flow," similar to the super-rich way, for an enhanced retirement lifestyle. Now, who is considered to be a super rich individual?

A definition for the *super rich* is:

For some, cash flow is millions of dollars per year.

For some, cash flow is millions of dollars per month.

For some, cash flow is millions of dollars per week.

and, hold on tight!

For some, cash flow is millions of dollars per day.

You will learn in chapter four that for some super-rich people, the net operating retirement income (NORI) equals cash flow (CF).

The IRS defines passive activity income as:

> "Passive activity income includes all income from passive activities, and generally includes gain from disposition of an interest in a passive activity or property used in a passive activity."

The IRS defines rental activity as:

> "A rental activity is a passive activity, even if you materially participated in that activity. An activity is a rental activity if tangible property (real or personal) is used by customers or held for use by customers, and the gross income (or expected gross income) from the activity represents amounts paid (or to be paid) mainly for the use of the property. It does not matter whether the use is under a lease, a service contract, or some other arrangement."

Some examples of passive activity income are:

- Rental incomes (passive stream of retirement incomes [PSORI])
- Banked money (CD and money markets)
- Capital gains (on profit made from business sales)
- Dividends (gain from stocks and bonds)
- Sale of retail products (income from business activity)

Clearly, a *day job* is not a passive activity.

In the business of real estate as my retirement time-tested device, it is imperative to get a handle on the passive stream of retirement income (PSORI), which is the only option available to the middle class to gain access to generations and generations of wealth with little or no associated risk. Most, if not all, rookie investors are looking for property appreciation to make them rich in a short amount of time. However, I view this as a means of gaining access to my PSORI. The latter is more rewarding than the former in the long run. PSORI is the main stream revenue generator to properly fund our retirement. The best revenue value is achieved by accomplishing the gold standard secret of this treasured book. This view is clearly held by fast-food chains like McDonald's, KFC, Burger King, Jack in the Box, and others. They occupy prime locations, but are not looking to make quick bucks via real-estate appreciation. They are in it for the long haul. In fact, they are there to make money slowly and steadily over time. They want to buy retirement money machines that create generations and generations of wealth. Short-term gain (appreciation) is not the name of the game for them, nor is it for us. Most real-estate investment seminars and books encourage rapid buying and selling of property. Buy low and sell high is their mantra. When push comes to shove, most investors are merely looking for a cash cow or to strike gold in real estate deals. Some preach about scooping up bargains. Certainly, I agree that a lot of investors have made a ton of money by buying low and later, after adding some percent of forced appreciation to the property, selling high.

Icing on the Cake Inflation Hedge Secret

In real estate acquisitions, the buy-and-hold concept relies on the principle of location, location, location (or time), and its retirement income (revenue), not appreciation per se, or the underlying property value at any given time. Similarly, we are using real estate as our retirement tool to gain access to PSORI. As time advances, the PSORI goes up as we increase rents (to meet fair market rates), and as we lower the debt service (DS) and ultimately pay it off, thereby attaining the gold standard secret. Increasing rental income to fair market rents every year or two is our ultimate hedge against retirement inflation, and this is what I call *the icing on the cake inflation hedge secret* of our sustained retirement success. While traditional retirement portfolios often include fixed dollar amounts of the annuity checks, it is no match to our device, which comes with our choosing a predetermined amount (the lifestyle we choose) and, of course, with a *built-in inflation allowance.* We will be fully in command (being in captain's seat) of our PSORI ship from the very first voyage to its final destination is indeed our—retirement innovation engine—the key thrust feature that propels our desire to clench retirement wealth in achieving financial freedom, if not financial success as we would expect. For that reason, our generous financial ambition holds a very gratifying future. This certainly harmonizes with the title, *Generations and Generations of Wealth,* which is waiting for you, not just for the asking, but for the doing. This essentially is the icing on the cake inflation hedge and fringe benefit secret message.

Please pause reading here to consider the point.

Receiving Lump-sum Disbursement

If you are close to retiring and have elected to receive a lump-sum of your retirement money, one million dollars or so, please, please do not give it to some rookie stock broker or to some naïve financial planner who has no concrete knowledge of what the super rich have established for the middle class. I judge these people cannot be trusted. These people are inclined to rise to the challenge, because they care deeply about their share of the corporate proceeds—not ours. I desperately choose not to be in hot water. Please do not do anything that will jeopardize your retirement income and wealth.

Do not even discuss it with friends and relatives. Remember, everyone is hungry for a piece of that hot pie. Sometimes, though, they do not realize or care that this is your earnest retirement money that should support you in your golden years. I tell you, you may never again see this amount of money in your lifetime. So, please, please be extra, extra careful. For now, the only safe place is in a bank with closed doors. That is, rather than overextend your retirement nest egg and rush into making a high-priced decision, you may be better off, for now, staying put comfortably within your means and saving your cash for a down payment toward the purchase of real estate. Having said that, my best advice is: it's best to keep your money unshackled, out of harm's way, and accessible in the bank for the perfect opportunity when it comes along.

If you want a thing done well, do it yourself. I say, seize the golden opportunity and create your own retirement safety-net. Pay strict attention to my inspirational and educational teachings thoroughly and become a master builder of passive stream of retirement income (PSORI) for generations and generations to come. I know it's more easily said than done, but in time you'll be glad you followed my moneyed advice. I know I have the strength to survive and be there; I have tested it, worked out the kinks, and validated the PSORI concept.

Real Estate Appreciation

The key ingredient of this retirement plan is the passive stream of retirement income (PSORI) for creating generations and generations of wealth, even if the value of my property never goes up (zero appreciation). I consider my real estate a long-term retirement PSORI investment. Historically, long-term investments in real estate have tended to increase in value even in the midst of short ups and downs of the cyclical process. It is a very long-term investment. Remember, appreciation can be ignored simply because we'll never sell the goose that lays the golden eggs in our golden years, and we will, in fact, pass it on to our loved ones via a living trust. Appreciation is not the way to gain retirement income, whereas cash flow (CF) alone is. Did you understand and appreciate this appreciation point?

Inspirational Confidence Building

"To me nothing is worth more than what this book is trying to make me do. Every morning I am handed twenty-four golden hours. They are one of the few things in this world that I get free of charge. If I had all the money in the world, I couldn't buy an extra hour. What will I do with this priceless treasure?"

—Anonymous

"Knowing is not enough; we must apply. Willing is not enough; we must do."

—Johann W. V. Goethe

"The secret of success in life is for a person to be ready for opportunity when it comes."

—Benjamin Disraeli

"If you can dream it, you can do it."

—Walt Disney

"I was born into it and there was nothing I could do about it. It was there, like air or food, or any other element. The only question with wealth is what you do with it."

—John D. Rockefeller

Chapter 3

Developing a Retirement Plan

A POWERFUL RETIREMENT BUILDING PLAN

Many middle-class Americans believe that their retirement system is faced with major dilemmas. Americans are now living longer and spending more years in retirement than ever before, so our bank savings and retirement investments will need to last longer. It's becoming increasingly clear that without the personal dedicated efforts of most middle-class Americans to adequately fund themselves in their golden years, they will run into the risk of financial woe and exhaustion of funds. Even at full retirement age, they may have insufficient funds to cover the basic necessities of life and will intolerably be resigned to retiring broke or in poverty. Most will face the dire consequences of this retirement journey. This poses one of our country's most pressing challenges. And many baby boomers will have very little saved for their retirement nest egg due to poor-performing stock markets. Their vision, their dream for comfortable retirement, is not a reality. And also, at the end of the day, Americans began to sense the need to be of assistance to their loved ones who will be struggling to make a living in their golden years.

Remember, when we were children, we played with toys to mimic the nurse or the truck driver, and eventually we became a member of the working class. The super-rich owners of corporate America are keeping a lot of secrets from the middle class. They have the flexibility to do so. They set the standards. They even set the policy for the education system too, not to teach us (middle-class people) about finance (saving, investment, emergency cash cushion, so on, and so forth). Young adults taking college-level courses are usually not well trained in such topics, and, as a result, many ultimately end up in the middle class group. The super rich have programmed us to acquire education for twenty to thirty years and then programmed us to perform a day job for another thirty to forty years until we drop. Most college and university students think that higher education is the key answer to gaining access to wealth and hope to one day enjoy the super-rich lavish lifestyle. They expect that through education they will be sitting pretty, earning more than their parents, adequately raising a family, living in finer homes and neighborhoods, driving nicer cars, investing more wisely, saving for well-planned retirements, and being able to afford vacations to exotic places. The truth of the matter is that most of them will end up in the middle class and remain there throughout their lives. It's so touching. It's so striking. They become nine-to-five workers with little time for family and personal life. Their nifty expectations and witty dreams don't match reality, leading to dissatisfaction. This is what the super rich are doing to us: the middle class. Unfortunately, most present wage earners have chosen or will choose to work until they can no longer physically do so. I thought we paid our dues, and now it is time to cash in. Retirement is a time for vacations, a time for reflection, a time for receiving rewards, and a time for enjoying life. Does society really care about individuals like us? Not really. Basically, you are on your own with little escape from government retirement mandates. But we can overcome these retirement hurdles, dilemmas, and financial cataclysms.

I believe ours is the one exceptional way to hedge being poverty-stricken for longevity. Our business of retirement innovation is the key and a continual process. Sustained success of my business plan is based on proper management of my cash flow. The big question is, how can you learn from failures if you have not tried to succeed? Well, my success has been tested by me and is fail proof and enduring. It has been said, "Learn from your failures." Yes, I say, I learned success from my failures. The glitches have been removed. And finally the process has been validated. This system demonstrates how your retirement life can be changed for the better. Be my associate. Yes, please be my associate and duplicate my efforts, my experiences, in reaching the gold standard secret. This is an inspirational and educational book, and its wisdom and strong advice is like taking a college course with a college professor teaching at the high school level. By the way, no college professor's audacious and empowering lectures will make you rich, but this valuable book's compelling wisdom will accomplish the mighty trick, if you are willing to apply its valiant lessons.

These are teachings from my personal experience in becoming rich and passing these riches down the pipeline to my descendants. A number of principles discussed here will overlap from time to time, which will help to reinforce the message and to motivate us. Bear in mind that repetition is the key to learning these life-changing principles. I hope you will learn the underlying principles and never, ever forget them. I hope that you quickly learn what took me years to master by trial and error. Please commit to memory that in real-estate investment there is rarely instant gratification, especially for those who are unwilling to work hard. Please know that time should heal any investment dents in real estate, even if you purchased property at prevailing fair market value. It is the PSORI with cash flow that I am looking for. I pride myself on this and so will you.

It's just like when your mom or dad cooked a delicious dinner. Their satisfaction came when the dinner was enjoyed with their taste buds, filling to capacity and they received compliments. Similarly, I will be grateful when you accomplish your retirement dream, i.e., creating generations and generations of wealth investing in a duplex, a triplex, or a fourplex real estate and later achieving the gold standard secret of this powerful clear-thinking retirement-building plan. The secret lies in being an early bird in your retirement planning and wealth building. And a sincere willingness to learn a few glorious and radiant inspirational confidence building as we march on this innovative empowering retirement journey. Most folks would say, "Go ahead; push me into doing something good for a change." Yes, certainly I concur, a little push and a little inspiration toward wealth building will go a long way and will do the most sought-after mighty trick. I dreamed of having a retirement income plan where only a few people would know, being a so-called "silent" business entrepreneur. Or running it under a fictitious business name. Now, without realizing it, I have become a—silent business owner. The secret message is, merely owning a piece of real estate and renting it, I have the opportunity to run it and watch it with a muted owner name. It's up and running under a business name. My dream is a reality now. This is what I call my *silent entrepreneur secret.* And my melting pot under a dba (doing business as) is brimming with cash flow from passive steam of retirement income. Ironically, it is a recipe for hardship in seeking for wealth building, especially in your golden years, if you are not actually making money.

Goal Setting for the Small Business

Goal setting for a prolonged can-do attitude is the key to owning the small business. Because it is a long, long-term commitment, it may be one of the hardest things about real estate retirement investing. Please, treasure up in the memory that you simply don't make retirement money on real estate you don't own. Simple as that. Somebody else is. What could be better than having a complete business plan and a complete retirement plan in one? We can kill two birds with one stone. It's our best two-piece satisfaction system. What's the best kept secret? Is it just owning a duplex, a triplex, or a fourplex? I know a number of Californians, including myself, who purchased their first fourplex that initially had a negative cash flow, say, $500 to as much as $1000/mo. But after a year, they turned it into positive cash flow. How did they do it? By refinancing the mortgage at a lower rate and by increasing the rent to fair market level. While knowing that you are working for your retirement sanctuary, which comes with a prolonged joy for you and your loved ones, please get a grip on yourself in pursuing it vigorously with a specific due date. Just grin and bear it—owning and renting a piece of real estate is a business just like the super rich's business. Keep it a secret. Be happy deep down in your heart that you have a plan, a business plan, sure enough—a small business plan (to be more specific). Yes, it's a secret business plan. And the best part is no one will know unless you disclose it, even when it is up and running. A secret business plan that the super rich already have, that when placed in operation, generates indisputable revenue (rental income) for the remainder of your life and beyond. It's possible to generate a never-ending passive stream of retirement income (PSORI), to supplement or replace our lost retirement annuity. Believe me. It is sturdy, reliable, and lucrative. This is what I call the *generations and generations of wealth secret.* Sustained success of our business plan is based on cash flow from PSORI. And hold in mind that this will not only give your lost retirement annuity check back to you but will create generations and generations of wealth for you and your loved ones too.

The super rich teach their loved ones how to maintain their super rich status. We, in the middle class group, need to properly instill our retirement investment ideas in our loved ones so that they too can foster wealth accumulation throughout their lives. This should be initiated from childhood to adulthood. Let us plant the seeds that will grow and preserve our values in future generations. It's a challenge in life to take care of our loved ones, isn't it? Well, your family thinking will change, being rich and happy at the same time. I believe wealth can bring happiness in my life if I know how to prospect and respect it. This book predominately values the middle class, the working class, i.e., you and I, and this will certainly bring us more in line with the super rich's secret money making methods. A subconscious mind-set business plan from a conscious mind-set should be in the making to bring much needed wealth and entranced happiness in our retirement years.

For an ideal goal setting, I recommend the following: (1) motivate yourself by learning some of the inspirational confidence building, (2) fill in the *author's appreciation* section, (3) set a date of purchase and a date of attaining the gold standard secret (between seven to fifteen years), (4) choose a plan of action—with a dedicated aim setting—four units, three units, two units, (5) learn *all* the real-time support and execution (wisdom of this book). This is what I call a *creditable goal-setting secret.* So, please let's roll up our sleeves and get down to business.

The Nifty Amenities of Real Estate as the Retirement Investment Tool

As for the best of times and the worst of times, the best of retirement times are over for some Americans, and regretfully, the worst of times are here to stay for the majority. I believe that this book's guidance should bring the best of times back again and more. Investment in stocks is, in fact, giving our hard-earned money to someone who works for a big corporation, thinking they will return to us more than we give them. This may turn out not to be true. Traditionally, stock market investment may have been a way to boost retirement income for a lot of folks, but it's still a far cry from where it used to be; tragically, it is by no means the main determinant of achieving wealth. To me, it's like putting my retirement money in a slot machine to get a return. No way! Fat chance! It's like being under the sun without proper attire and head gear. The truth is I want to reverse this. I want my tenants to put their money in my own one-way trading machine, and then I can say, "Ah! It is in my retirement account."

We should think of our duplex or triplex or fourplex as our one-way trading machine, forever creating generations and generations of wealth. Keep an open mind for retirement investments, take advantage of opportunities around you, and ultimately you can accomplish a lot, even in your golden years from your home-based business. I decide how I want to reach my planned goals, but I still follow my tested steps, which come with little or no risk. To be unprepared in our golden years is like planting the best crops without watering them.

I guarantee that you will surely but gradually make it by cash-flow ownership and working hard at your day job to finally pay off your duplex or triplex or fourplex. You are certainly not going to do what other real-estate investors did or are doing by being greedy for equity growth, called appreciation. Others failed because they took too much risk. How? They overleveraged a purchase by making little or no down payment and signing an adjustable rate mortgage (ARM) through sub-prime lending. Of course, some may have been the victims of job layoffs and could not keep up with the mortgage payments. They did 90 to 100 percent financing, and so the mortgage payments were too high. If I go for 100 percent borrowing, I would have to use dual financing (primary and secondary) with so-called first and second loans. The second loan is very costly since the lender is in second place in the event I default. Therefore, the second loan mortgage rate will be a great deal higher compared to the first loan.

Some investors fail due to naïvety. They may have read too many books that preached 100 percent financing, by using other people's money (OPM) to become rich via high leveraging. Books with titles like *Achieve Big with No Money Down, Buy Low Sell High, Quick Wealth,* so on and so forth, inspired them to make the erroneous move. No doubt some people made fortunes by sheer luck: being in the right place at the right time. Or, in actuality, they worked hard, experienced some failures along the way, but ultimately succeeded. One hundred percent financing is the root cause of the problem. Above all, these people had little or no knowledge of proper landlord duties and also no knowledge of keeping some funds in reserve (emergency cash cushion) in case of money woes. Satan drove them down the wrong path. Because of a low or no down payment obsession, the acquired property suffered from negative cash flow. These investors were slapped with an unbearably large negative cash flow each month, which ultimately led to their downfall. Remember, it is the proper management of cash flow from the very initiation point (date of purchase) that is the secret to the sustained success of our small business for our retirement revenue. It is the over-leveraged property that can be problematic.

Real estate is cyclical. If the real estate cycle gets so grim that I cannot afford my vacancy rate, I lower my rent to attract tenants from the surrounding vicinity. Because I have positive cash flow, I have a cushion to run a successful small real-estate business. Again the secret is that I can easily compete in my region for the fair market rent. Our system of government is, of course, deeply rooted in the principle of capitalism, which permits competition in an ideal open market. My point is, even with competition, we will always win. Do you see this powerful secret? We will always win this retirement innovation. This is what I call the *cutting-edge competition secret.* Please store in mind that now we have the similar flexibility just like the super rich. If truth be told, ours is a one-way winning progressive slot machine! Please be acquainted with the business of retirement innovation, based on a solid foundation commencing from the very acquisition (cash flow purchase) of our money making machine to the very end-to-end. By owning a fourplex, I realized I could swim with the sharks and never get eaten. So, you see, I am best equipped to deal with the foreseeable credit crunch debacle or financial fiasco. Within two decades, the number of persons age sixty-five and over will nearly double. The population is always increasing, and a basic necessity of living is housing, especially a duplex or a triplex or a fourplex, where the nifty amenities are comparable to a single family residence (SFR).

Tally of Nifty Amenities of Real Estate Retirement Investments:

(1) Cash flow
(2) Tax benefits/shelter
(3) Tax depreciation deduction
(4) Equity growth from Mortgage loan reduction
(5) Appreciation
(6) Leverage

List of Advantages to Owning a Fourplex:

(1) Easy to care for; a resident manager is not needed
(2) Easy to turn around and it still falls in the same category as SFR, therefore financing is similar to SFR (Note: five or more units is considered a commercial apartment complex.)
(3) Tax advantages are more than SFR (e.g., tax claim operating expenses)

(4) It is a housing crisis hedge since those having problems with SFR will rent it

(5) We can still claim homestead exemption for property tax if we reside in one of the units

(6) Unlike large multiunit properties, here our tenants pay for almost all operating expenses including water, garbage, gas, and electric

(7) Best of all, we can attain the gold standard secret (free-and-clear title) if we set our mind to it, and therefore we can retire early and being rich from our day job.

I first started out with SFRs but swiftly learned that cash flow is always in the negative territory. In fact, with my three SFRs, I ended up having too much negative cash flow; however, I turned it around after a year via refinancing and increasing the rents to fair market rate. I got lucky because the feds lowered the mortgage rates.

Building Wealth as the Super Rich Do

For Super Rich, CF = Expandable Retirement Income
For some Super Rich, NORI = Expandable Retirement Income

Cash flow is simply defined as the surplus money remaining from a business activity for the super rich to enjoy, i.e., money left over for the super rich after paying all the operating expenses (OE) of their business transactions each month. This is cash to keep or spend as they wish. Cash flow is also called expandable retirement income for the super rich. You'll learn later that for some super rich net operating retirement income (NORI) is their expandable retirement income. The source of expandable retirement income initially comes from a passive stream of retirement income (PSORI) also called gross schedule retirement rental income. (Realtors call it gross expandable rental income or gross schedule rental income, or simply gross rental income.) After paying annual operating expenses (OE), I get my annual net operating retirement income (NORI), and then after paying my annual debt service (DS), I get my cash flow (CF). CF is normally reported as an annual figure (multiply it by twelve).

Mini Cash Flow Analysis Form

Transaction	**Monthly**	**Yearly**
Passive Stream of Retirement Income (PSORI) or (Gross Schedule Retirement Rental Income)		
Less Operating Expenses (OE)		
Net Operating Retirement Income (NORI)		
Less Debt Service (DS)		
Cash Flow (CF) = Expandable Retirement Income		

Sample Cash Flow Formula

$$CF = NORI_{(a)} - DS_{(a)}$$

CF = Cash flow; NORI = Net Operating Retirement Income; DS = Debt Service; $_{(a)}$= Annual

For the super rich, cash flow is one of the main sources of expandable retirement income for retirement, and, of course, for some it is net operating retirement income (NORI). For the most part, the super rich inherit this wisdom from their parents and pass it to their children in the state of subconscious mind-set. They ensure that their subconscious mind-set is well programmed through conscious mind-set with the new business of retirement innovation at birth to adulthood. Their parents do a superb job of programming. One of the best-kept secret programs of the super rich is that, unlike the middle class, they are "born retired" and so are free from day-job obligations. You see, one of the clear differences between the super rich and the middle class is that the super rich are so well programmed and organized that they give their inheritance wealth up front, whereas the middle class give up their inheritance wealth when they die! It's so tragic!

Please pause reading here to consider the point.

Beautiful Relationship

I say, give the wealth now while you are alive and well or at least share the wisdom of family wealth building just as you share your food, house, car, so on and so forth with your loved ones. Help the loved ones with a down payment and teach the retirement scheme set forth herein. For this one, please don't keep it a secret. Please share the wisdom of this book with your loved ones. I suggest that you purchase one copy of this retirement innovation book for each loved one to use as a permanent reference for years and years to come as they grow with the plan. And above all, their subconscious mind-set will be well programmed as they grow with a clear conscious mind-set. Tell them about your clear-cut and long-established action plan and be involved in building a beautiful, beautiful relationship. This is what I call *permanent reference and beautiful relationship secret.* For this I would say, "Please, God, bless this family for sharing information, the way you, God, want it."

Expandable Retirement Income Is Truly the Spendable Retirement Income Secret

The super rich never really undertake a day job. They have their own money-making machine (business) to give them the expandable retirement income (ERI). (Realtors call it expandable rental income or simply expandable income.) The question is, when can a day job worker (middle class) say, "I am ready to retire from the day job"? I remember numerous folks provided me with the same answer by saying, "Keep giving me my monthly day-job paycheck, and I will gladly retire early." I have learned from the wisdom of this book that the super rich have already received that day-job paycheck at "birth," and therefore consider themselves "born retired." Unlike the middle class, the super rich ideally don't work for the purpose of making a living. In fact, their businesses work for them by providing that paycheck called cash flow. After paying all the operating expenses (OE) and debt service (DS), if any, they get the cash flow (CF) and for some net operating retirement income (NORI) is their expandable retirement income (ERI). This is what defines and honors super rich status and gives them their daily bread and status called *spendable* retirement income (SRI). (Realtors call it spendable rental income or spendable income.) This is too good to be true. Needless to say, it is! This is what I call our *spendable retirement income secret.*

Please pause reading here for a moment and think about the secret you just learned.

____

____

____

The Super Rich's Loved Ones are "Born Retired"

Mind you, their genetic makeup coupled with this business of retirement innovation ensures preservation of financial resources for generations and generations of wealth to come. As a matter of fact, the super rich go to school to socialize with the middle class (working class) and learn to scout for good prospective day workers and, of course, to learn the retirement business. Yes, now I remember someone did ask me when I was a student at University of California Berkeley, "Would you like to work for my father's firm? He will pay you well. He is looking for a genius like you." He gave me his father's business card, but I never called him. Instead, I ended up working for the U. S. Food and Drug Administration (FDA) in the San Francisco District as a recall and emergency coordinator. Because the super rich know retirement tricks of the trade, they never become lawyers or doctors or engineers. Did Donald Trump or Bill Gates or Warren Buffet tell their children to go to school and become non-business professionals (lawyers or doctors or engineers)? Fat chance! Certainly not! For each child, they set up a business empire based in a breathtaking home or from their conspicuous powerful office. They are leaders by virtue of being wealthy, something most of us just dream of. And they produce wealthy children from a conscious mind-set to subconscious mind-set.

Now, please let me conclude here by giving you a delicious, delicious dessert after finishing the main course (for reading up to this point). Okay, ready. Promise me you'll pause reading and ponder for a minute or two. Please don't say, "Oh! Don't give me that again." Well, I thank you so much and may God bless you.

Okay, I said earlier one of the secret programs of the super rich is that their loved ones are *born retired* and therefore are free from day-job obligations, unlike the middle class. And remember from chapter two, when I told you about our ultimate retirement elements or expectations. Let me rewrite it in *italics* so that you don't have to refer back and forth.

A general definition that most of us understood, or thought we believed by observing our grandparents and/or our parents retire from their day jobs, would include the following desired elements or retirement expectations:

- *A pension, either a lump-sum payment or monthly annuity check*
- *A paid-off mortgage on a primary residence*
- *Adequate savings and possibly a second home as a retirement investment*
- *Adequate insurance coverage (medical and life) that is wholly or at least partly subsidized by the former employer*
- *Time to travel and see new places*
- *Time to spend time with loved ones*
- *Time to get closer to God*
- *Time to relax, reflect, entertain, and enjoy hobbies*

A super rich's child has enough golden eggs in the basket, and their portfolio is well diversified. The child's wealth is enough to survive many ups and downs in the economy. The child is sitting pretty, having all of the above desired elements or expectations and more. Can you think of anything else the child has? Here are some things:

- The child is free at home and the office (like a retired grandpa).
- The child discovers he/she is different from the others, i.e., the child sees daily chores being done by someone else in the house and the office.

- The child sees and sits on a grand chair at the office and home.
- The child is admired by everyone, including the media and TV folks and feels admired by everyone he/she sees.
- The child learns to thank God, instead of begging.
- The child learns to share his wealth with the poor (alms giving).
- The child travels by business class.
- Above all, the child's health is well guarded. The child lives well, eats well, sleeps well, puts on good clothes, looks good, smells good, exercises under nurse guidance, perceives everything as beautiful, and is well admired and nurtured. Therefore, the brain rejuvenates well and, of course, the subconscious mind-set is well programmed through conscious mind-set under fabulous surroundings.

What do I conclude from the preceding bullets?

Well, I conclude that the super rich's child is retired as my wife's grandpa retired. The child is not only pleased with God's blessings but learns to thank God regularly. The child learns to scout good people to work for his/her father's firm, thereby providing employment to the middle class and also learns to give alms to the needy and the poor with no concern for wealth depletion, since the child perceives a land of plenty. The child never plans for vacation like the middle class. As a matter of fact, the child is constantly on "vacation" status. The child takes frequent business class trips to other places in the world, like Fiji Islands, Hawaii, Puerto Rico, Dubai, Canada, London, and other places of business. The child learns that the IRS allows his/her parents to claim certain vacation expenses as business deductions since the parents have businesses to conduct around the world. The child learns that his/her parents perform special (extra) prayers at night, not to beg God, but to thank him. Yes, the child's subconscious mind-set is well prepared to love, cherish, and enjoy the beautiful earth through God's blessing. The child learns to prepare for the next world to meet God and to show him the faith he/she had and all the good deeds he/she did while on earth. The best part is the blessed child learned from the super-rich parent's wisdom and advice to always thank God by saying: Halleluiah, Alham-du-lilla, Boruch Hashem, Jai Bhagwan/Namaste, Salamat Sa Diyos, Alabar a Dios, Gan xie shen/Gum ger suen (Praise the God, or all praise belongs to God, or blessed be God).

As you promised me, please pause reading here and contemplate what we should be doing to set a precedent for ourselves.

I know you already know the answer. In short, buy a fourplex and change the subconscious mind-set to attaining the gold standard secret of this book. Repeat the process for each loved one and you can ultimately create generations and generations of wealth. The rest is history. Folks, be an ambitious and generous parent and help your loved ones to retire rich too. For that I'll say many happy returns! May God bless you.

Inspirational Confidence Building

"The future belongs to those who believe in the beauty of their dreams."

—Eleanor Roosevelt

"Having a goal is a state of happiness."

—E. J. Bartek

"What we do not understand we do not posses."

—Johann W. V. Goethe

"Ideas without action are worthless."

—Harvey Mackay

"Every so often, life is like a box of chocolates, some of it is hard and some of it is soft, and you never know what's coming next, but all you can do is hope for the best."

—Mahtab S. Ali

Chapter 4

Acquiring Retirement Assets

PRINCIPLES OF BUYING AND HOLDING

Buying and holding the goose that lays golden eggs is the one option available to us, the middle class, for gaining access to a substantial and reliable source of sustained retirement income and success. The golden eggs are, in fact, the passive stream of retirement income (PSORI), which will support the creation of generations and generation of wealth. Working toward attaining the gold standard secret of this book will further enhance and guarantee generations and generations of wealth.

Many retirement investors have failed to recognize that a single family residence (SFR) is not the ideal way to achieve desired income for retirement. Personally, investing in SFRs is not my cup of tea. I clearly distinguish this approach from others, and I do not recommend having SFRs in my retirement portfolio. Why? Firstly, the fair market price to cash flow percentile is too low (assuming all cash purchase). Secondly, if the tenant moves out, we'll end up with 100 percent vacancy rate, whereas a fourplex would only have 25 percent vacancy rate upon the departure of one tenant. Simply put, for SFRs, we'll have to handle a large negative cash flow even with a sizable down payment toward the purchase. This is not the suitable method in creating retirement income, whereas a fourplex is.

Note: My associate should understand that because of the housing crisis, acquiring a fourplex, the gold standard, has increasingly discouraged many middle class from making such an investment. My top secret advice: avert this impeding financial debacle—be my innovator associate, and for now, use it to your advantage with less competition.

I remember as late as 1979, back then, California SFRs were affordable. A neighbor was essentially able to purchase another neighbor's house for rental income and did not get into financial misery, even if it sat vacant for three months or more. Basically, the neighbor bought the home to relieve the other, because they were close friends. If you put 20 percent down, you would have good cash flow. Back then most people did not regard an SFR as a retirement money machine, since the appreciation was not great, ranging from 2 to 4 percent per year. Most people bought a second house because their neighbor was moving and convinced them to purchase his/her house, a sort of prearranged transaction. Although the selling price was set at fair market level, the purchaser had to sign a thirty-year loan arrangement. If the neighbor could afford to make the mortgage payments, then it was an okay deal. Needless to say, they could not predict that the present-day market price would essentially double in a decade and then would double or more within a single year. Doubled or even more in a year! Get real! You would be rolling in dough. Bought it for $100,000 and sold it for $200,000 to $225,000 after holding it for just a year. Many of us were spoiled by a real estate market boom that appreciated at an exceedingly fast-pace, a whopping 100 to 125 annual percent increase in sale price in California. SFRs were the way to make quick bucks. You could make a killing. A lot of people became wealthy. Back then, $100,000 was a lot of money to me. SFR investing was hot and growing by leaps and bounds. You could easily strike it rich. Of course, as the market price kept going up and up and up, the buying frenzy eventually slowed. Now the neighbors cannot afford to buy each other's houses under any circumstances. If they did, there would be essentially no cash flow, huge negative to carry, even if you could afford to put 50 percent down. SFR acquisition for retirement income appeared iffy. For rookie investors, gone are the days when they could buy a house with little or no money down, and flip it after making some improvements. So, folks, SFRs are not the way to obtain annuity checks for retirement. Today, we buy an SFR as a place to reside, not as a means of retirement income. Of course, SFR's can turn out to be one of the best investments for some and can supply lump-sum retirement income when cashed-out, particularly when the seller is moving to a lower fair market price SFR region, or relocating to a region with a lower cost of living. This may be a viable option if you need more cash right away. Many Americans have done this because they had no choice but to cash out and move to a lower cost of living or a less desirable neighborhood.

Remember, this book covers the following in detail:

(1) Building wealth as the super rich do (Creating generations and generations of wealth.)

(2) Motivating by means of inspirational confidence building.

(3) Developing a passive stream of retirement income for life (PSORI).

(4) Eliminating the risk associated with the acquisition of duplexes, triplexes, or fourplexes (small business).

(5) Using down payment from your 401(k) or 403(b) retirement or thrift savings plan (TSP) federal government retirement plan, or best yet, derived from personal savings, and/or borrowing a portion from a rich uncle to purchase a duplex, triplex, or a fourplex.

(6) Achieving the gold standard and the gold standard secret of this book.

(7) Managing with the best property management tools.

(8) Overcoming investment fears.

(9) Creating wealth for loved ones.

(10) Being organized in life.

(11) Being conscious of God in your daily life through piety and alms.

(12) Enjoying the responsibility and life.

"The Beauty of a Life We Lived Became a Legacy … "

I learned something worthwhile from my wife's grandpa, who lived and retired in the city of South San Francisco, California, after working as a carpenter for nearly thirty years. We remember him for the exceptional work he did in helping to build a number of San Francisco landmarks, including the Bank of America headquarters and San Francisco International Airport. He began his career in 1966. On day one, he knew he had found a good job with decent salary and he vowed to work thirty years and then retire. While he knew his house would be paid off in the year 1996 (thirty-year fixed-rate mortgage), given his utmost discretion of savings for retirement, he nevertheless anticipated his annuity check to adequately fund him and his wife in their golden years. Besides working as a carpenter, he did something for which I now wholeheartedly admire him. His elegant legacy and inspiration toward wealth building lives on. His passion was to build a retirement money machine that would create generations and generations of wealth for himself and his loved ones. He built a gorgeous fourplex (gold standard) and attained the gold standard secret long before this book was ever conceived. Refresh your memory: to achieve the gold standard, an associate has to purchase a fourplex and work toward getting a free-and-clear title (gold standard secret). The building is still in the family today. My wife's grandpa left his beloved legacy on earth and went back to God in the year 2000. We cherish the memory of my wife's grandpa, in fact, his beloved commemorative plaque reads, "The beauty of a life we lived became a legacy that stays behind and warms the hearts, and every memory is today's strength that lives in our tomorrow's forever." May God bless him and Grandma too.

I learned from my wife's grandpa's life history that back then life in America was good and satisfying, but, best of all, it was predictable. When you retired in those days, everyone was there to help you, the bank gave back the promissory note with a free-and-clear title, and the employer gave you monthly annuity checks for life. You would have enough to get by. To escape the ordinary, we live in a different world today. Things have changed. For better or worse, you decide. But with the help of this book's wisdom and strong advice, we shall overcome and be better off than ever. Let's make up our minds and do it in support of this innovation.

Down Payment

Down payment = A Percentage of the Accepted Price

Question: Do we have the down payment to purchase the property? Yes, we do, or say, in time we will. The down payment is locked in our 401(k) or 403(b)—(for corporations), or in a TSP (Thrift Saving Plan—for federal government sector), or best yet, derived from personal savings, and/or borrowing a portion from a rich uncle to purchase the duplex, triplex, or fourplex. We do not have to take all the money out, just enough to purchase the property and with the guidance of this life-changing book, the rest is history. Or you may simply pledge to yourself, if you are just starting your day job, to work hard and save for the down payment. You may wish to engage in some creative financing, for example, borrowing some portion of equity from a relative's house as the down payment towards the purchase. If the relative is approachable and concurs, work with him/her in written agreeable terms, and you should, as a gesture of appreciation, promise to repay his/her equity payments for that portion until, in time, pay that off completely. For a quick start, this may be a very, very viable option for some whose rich uncle or aunt is impeccable for this undertaking. Your broker or sales agent may refer you to a lender for a pre-qualified loan. Please work with a lender prior to making the offer.

Understanding lenders questions pertaining to obtaining a loan obligation:

Mortgage Lender Questions: (Credit? Capacity? and Collateral?)

- Credit: Am I financially stable and reliable (FICO score)?
- Capacity: What kind of outstanding debt do I already owe? Do I have enough earning power and net worth to repay the loan?

- Collateral: Do I own any other property that can be promised to a lender to guarantee full payment of loan?

Understanding FICO Scores

A FICO Score is a credit score, a number that lenders use to measure credit risk or creditworthiness of a borrower by looking at a borrower's credit report. FICO is a registered trademark of Fair Isaac Corporation. In the US and Canada, the major consumer reporting agencies are: (1) TransUnion, (2) Equifax, and (3) Experian.

Categorizing FICO Scores:

- Over 720—Excellent
- 680–720—Very Good
- 620–680—Borderline
- 620-below—Not Good

I have used more of my hard-earned money from my Thrift Savings Plan (TSP) federal government retirement account, comparable to 401(k) or 403(b), to finance deals. I have put 20 to 40 percent down payments toward financing the deals with positive cash flows, of course. This is the main reason I did not become a high-risk retirement business owner. Just imagine, if you bought a duplex, triplex, or a fourplex outright with cash, using funds from your 401(k) or 403(b) or Thrift Savings Plan (TSP) federal government retirement account, you wouldn't have any mortgage payment. You'd never run into the sub-prime debacle. The title will be yours free and clear. Whoopee! Splendid! You would reward yourself by embarking on a fabulous vacation to the Fiji

Islands, landing at the Nadi International Airport, a recognition you deserve. You are on your way to creating generations and generations of wealth. I'd express my gratitude to that end and pronounce many happy returns, and I'd say: Halleluiah, Alham-dulilla, Boruch Hashem, Jai Bhagwan/Namaste, Salamat Sa Diyos, Alabar a Dios, Gan xie shen/Gum ger suen (Praise the God, or all praise belongs to God, or blessed be God).

Use Internet Figures for Success

I locate prime retirement income properties and use Internet figures for success. Using Internet information for guidance is one of the best ways to find an ideal duplex, triplex, or a fourplex property to purchase. It always helps me to search for the specific listings in a particular region. It is one of the fastest road maps to effective communications. Not only does it provide loads of useful information, including the site maps, snap shot photos, or virtual tours of the property, but it allows me to work from the comfort of home without any outside pressure in deciding what and where to make a purchase offer. Most importantly, I get to work with the figures provided in the listing, namely, the seller's income and expense statement, allowing me to prepare my preliminary offer by using our "Paramount Property–Purchase Offer–Analysis Form" before its formal presentation to the listing agent and the seller. I can even get the listing agent's telephone number and have a little chitchat, asking if the property is still available and a host of other pertinent questions. This is the best of the best preparations that the best and the brightest use to make the right purchase offer. Using online information and asking pertinent questions to the listing agent is what I call the *www.RetireLucky.com secret.*

Once you have accumulated enough for a down payment, from 401(k) or 403(b) plan, or Thrift Savings Plan (TSP) federal government retirement plan or, best yet, derived from personal savings and/or borrowing a portion from a rich uncle, you are a *ready, willing,* and *able* buyer from my perspective, because herein I provide you with all of the necessary tools to accomplish the acquisition. I use these mathematical calculations to see precisely where I fit in the picture. My offers are based on figures that I can clearly see. One million dollars has six zeros. It's a figure. Being wealthy is a figure. Just imagine, earning $83,333 per month approximately equates to $1,000,000 per year. Know how to figure and come up with the correct number (answer). Figuratively speaking, for example, I learned from my physics class that $E = MC^2$ (Albert Einstein's mass-energy formula) and it is a figure. I believe God made the whole world based on figures, and the whole universe is based on mathematical calculations called figures. Figures tell the truth and remain constant unless I change them. Our small business runs on figures. We live in a digital age. Figuratively, it gives me a very clear answer of the anticipated profitability of my small business investment account. Figures do not lie. In fact, figures could tell a great, great divine story. Again, I wonder if God uses figures to envisage the outcome of his creations. God says, "Be it," and it is, and the laws of physics are followed.

The *caveat emptor* (let the buyer beware) norm should be a controlling criterion. Simply put, I know what I am buying. Buying the best is a good approach for us, because we are here for a *long, long, long* haul and to make the controlling idea here work for us, creating generations and generations of wealth. So, to get an offer accepted, I may offer fair market price, even though most sellers ask for top dollar. Although, I know you may have competition for the best properties, I encourage you to buy the best. Please, keep the memory alive by knowing that we are not looking for rapid appreciation; we are looking for a passive stream of retirement income (PSORI). Conversely, if the numbers are against me, I can know this in advance. In an offer competition situation, never shell out more than the asking price. And never be the fall guy! I have learned this from my previous purchases in

California, that some negative cash flow initially is okay, assuming I did not put a sizable down payment toward the purchase. Future increases in rent will take care of it. In fact, just knowing what I am dealing with is vital to this decision-making process, and figures make it all possible. Cash flow figuring is uttermost crucial in the decision-making process. This is to be sure we have the facts straight before we make a decision. Making an informed decision should be a no-brainer through the wisdom of this book that follows next.

Now, please, please, I repeat please, fully bear with me here, brace yourself, get a firm grip, because this is where the hub of success will be based on, in this decision-making process of getting your hands on PSORI for life and creating generation and generations of wealth. This should actually remove the major, major investment fears that are commonly held by the middle class. Next, I will explain in detail the decision-making process that is paramount to making a purchase offer. I will fully discuss these criteria next. Okay, get inspired to weigh in your retirement investment that the best and the brightest use for clarity and in supporting retirement cash flow transparency. So, please read what follows carefully.

Paramount Property Purchase Offer Analysis

This chapter will attempt to answer the paramount question:

Buy or Not to Buy a particular retirement property, which should be based on figures first, and then, due diligence, and then, common sense. I say, test the waters by using my "Paramount Property Purchase Offer Analysis Form" before you jump the gun.

Always Buy with Small Computations—Best Litmus Test

In making real-estate purchase investment decisions big or small (big as a shopping mall or small as a duplex), the terms CR or cap rate (capitalization rate), COCR (cash-on-cash return),

DCR (debt coverage ratio), and GRM (gross rent multiplier) are controlling standards commonly used by investors, bankers, mortgage bankers and private lenders for assessing these risk criteria. These small simple mathematical formulas are the compelling reasons to buy or not to buy and can provide quick and accurate answers that most investors are looking for. We are educated and we ought to be able to crunch the numbers and make educated decisions, i.e., know the facts and figures, and then decide. We need accurate figures for our computation and not back-of-the-envelope calculations, because we are going to use our hard-earned money. Right? So let's make an educated offer and make better quality investment decisions with my best litmus test.

Firstly, let's learn to use CR (cap rate), COCR, DCR, and GRM formulas in an ideal case study and then expand the same case study to include detailed information of the figures, explanations and calculations for a $500,000 offer and also for a $900,000 offer.

Capitalization Rate (CR or Cap Rate)

Capitalization rate (CR or cap rate) is the rate of return on a retirement investment. In other words, it is a way of valuing a purchase offer of a property by use of the net operating retirement income (NORI), to the probability of finding the risk factor associated with a retirement investment. A cap rate is a property's expected annual NORI expressed as a percentage of a buyer's retirement investment. The cap rate is calculated by dividing annual NORI by the purchase price (value of property) and multiplying it by 100 to get a percentile.

Important note: cap rate only accounts for return from NORI and not from property appreciation. This is good! Since this milestone book does not consider property appreciation as a means of PSORI.

$$CR = \frac{NORI_{(a)}}{V} \times 100$$

CR = cap rate (%); NORI = net operating retirement income
V = value (of property);
$_{(a)}$ = annual

Cash-on-Cash Return (COCR)

A calculation that gives me a percent return (profit) on my investment to the *cash* I contributed toward my investment. First, I calculate the cash flow (CF), NORI subtract DS, and then I divide it by the acquisition cost (AC) and multiply it by 100. To get percent of COCR, the formula appears below:

COCR:

$$CF = NORI_{(a)} - DS_{(a)}$$

$$COCR = \frac{CF}{AC} \times 100$$

COCR = cash-on-cash return; CF = cash flow; NORI = net operating retirement income; DS = debt service; $_{(a)}$ = annual; AC = acquisition cost

Debt Coverage Ratio (DCR)

DCR is a ratio of annual net operating retirement income ($NORI_{(a)}$) to annual debt service ($DS_{(a)}$). It measures annual $NORI_{(a)}$ relative to annual $DS_{(a)}$. Remember, debt service (DS) is another fancy word for mortgage payments that lenders like to use when they are evaluating the risk factor. It is mostly used by loan officers and underwriters when offering us a loan. The DCR is a powerful ratio figure that shows strength of cash flow. DCR of one clearly shows the break-even point, where there is neither positive cash flow nor negative cash flow. DCR of 2.00 shows strong cash flow, whereas 0.50 shows a negative cash flow. The DCR ratio formula appears below:

$$DCR = \frac{NORI_{(a)}}{DS_{(a)}}$$

DCR 0.50 = Negative CF
DCR 1.00 = *Break even*
DCR 2.00 = Strong CF

DCR = debt coverage ratio; NORI = net operating retirement income; $_{(a)}$ = annual; DS = debt service; CF = cash flow

Gross Rent Multiplier (GRM)

GRM is used to compare selling prices over annual rental incomes of similar listed properties for bargain hunting. GRM measures the selling price (SP) relative to the annual passive stream of retirement income ($PSORI_{(a)}$); i.e., a calculation that gives me SP price to ($PSORI_{(a)}$) ratio.

Important note: Most investors indicate GRM is a meaningless indicator, although it may make sense during a comparison with other similar listed properties for sale in a particular region. It appears in listings. So, it is better to know the term and its implied meaning. If a calculation equals a GRM of ten, it indicates sale price is ten times the $PSORI_{(a)}$.This tells me that a low GRM indicates a low selling price or vice versa. We may conclude that the lower the GRM the lower the selling price.

The GRM ratio formula appears below:

$$GRM = \frac{SP}{PSORI_{(a)}}$$

SP = selling price; GRM = gross rent multiplier; PSORI = passive stream of retirement income; $_{(a)}$ = annual

How to calculate net operating retirement income (NORI):

NORI is retirement revenue before making mortgage payments. (Realtors call it net operating rental income or net operating income, or simply, net income.)

I calculate my NORI by first finding my total passive stream of retirement income (PSORI) for the month, also called gross schedule retirement rental income. After paying operating expenses (OE) incurred for the month, I get my NORI. I multiply by twelve to get my annual figure.

NORI formula appears below:

$$NORI_{(a)} = PSORI_{(a)} - OE_{(a)}$$

NORI = net operating retirement income; PSORI = passive stream of retirement income; OE = operating expenses; $_{(a)}$ = annual

An Ideal Case Study

How to Calculate Capitalization Rate (Cap Rate or CR):

Cap Rate

$$CR = \frac{NORI_{(a)}}{V} \times 100$$

$CR_{(\%)}$ we desire = 6–12%

CR = cap rate (%); NORI = net operating retirement income; V = value (of property); $_{(a)}$ = annual

Assuming all cash transactions, suppose, a fourplex is projected to have $61,452 in $NORI_{(a)}$ this year. If my purchase offer was accepted for $500,000, the cap rate would be 12.29%. I consider this to be a best CR.

$$CR = \frac{\$61,452}{\$500,000} \times 100$$

$$CR = 12.29\%$$

Suppose, the same fourplex is projected to have \$56,592 in $NORI_{(a)}$ this year. If my purchase offer was accepted for \$900,000, the cap rate would be 6.29%. I consider this to be a low CR.

$$CR = \frac{\$56,592}{\$900,000} \times 100$$

CR = 6.29%

So this tells me that a low cap rate indicates a high selling price or vice versa. We can safely conclude that the higher the cap rate the lower the purchase price. Cap rates today might vary from four to fifteen, depending on your region, the length of existing tenants' leases, and fair market rents, low or high end.

How to calculate COCR (Cash-on-Cash Return):

COCR:

$$CF = NORI_{(a)} - DS_{(a)}$$

$$COCR = \frac{CF}{AC} \times 100$$

COCR we desire = 10–20%

COCR = cash-on-cash return; CF = cash flow; NORI = net operating retirement income; DS = debt service; $_{(a)}$ = annual; AC = acquisition cost

Suppose, the same fourplex is projected to have \$61,452 in annual $NORI_{(a)}$ this year with an annual mortgage payments of \$21,584 (DS) and having 6 percent fixed fully amortized thirty-year loan commitment. If my purchase offer was accepted for \$500,000 with an acquisition cost (forty percent down payment plus three percent closing costs) of \$215,000, the COCR would be 18.54%. I consider this to be the best return for the buck!

CF = \$61,452 – \$21,584 = \$39,868

$$COCR = \frac{\$39,868}{\$215,000} \times 100$$

COCR = 18.54%

Suppose the same fourplex is projected to have \$56,592 in $NORI_{(a)}$ this year with an annual mortgage payment of \$38,851 (DS) and having 6 percent fixed fully amortized thirty-year loan commitment. If my purchase offer was accepted for \$900,000 with an acquisition cost (40 percent down payment plus 3 percent closing costs) of \$387,000, the COCR would be 4.58%. This is a very low figure for COCR.

CF = \$56,592 – \$38,851 = \$17,741

$$COCR = \frac{\$17,741}{\$387,000} \times 100$$

COCR = 4.58%

How to calculate DCR (Debt Coverage Ratio):

DCR:

$$DCR = \frac{NORI_{(a)}}{DS_{(a)}}$$

DCR 0.50 = Negative CF
DCR 1.00 = *Break Even*
DCR 2.00 = Strong CF

DCR = debt coverage ratio; NORI = net operating retirement income; $_{(a)}$ = annual; DS = debt service; CF = cash flow

Suppose the same fourplex is projected to have \$61,452 in $NORI_{(a)}$ this year with an annual mortgage payment of \$21,584

(DS). If my purchase offer was accepted for $500,000, the DCR would be 2.85 indicating a strong CF.

$$DCR = \frac{\$61,452}{\$21,584}$$

DCR = 2.85

Suppose, the same fourplex is projected to have $56,592 in $NORI_{(a)}$ this year with annual mortgage payments of $38,851 (DS). If my purchase offer was accepted for $900,000, the DCR would be 1.46 indicating a moderate CF.

$$DCR = \frac{\$56,952}{\$38,851}$$

DCR = 1.46 (approx)

How to calculate GRM (gross rent multiplier):

$$GRM = \frac{SP}{PSORI_{(a)}}$$

SP = selling price; GRM = gross rent multiplier; PSORI = passive stream of retirement income; $_{(a)}$ = annual

Suppose, the same fourplex is projected to have $72,960 in $PSORI_{(a)}$ this year. If my purchase offer was accepted for $500,000, the GRM would be 6.85. Here the calculation depicts sale price is 6.85 times the $PSORI_{(a)}$.

$$GRM = \frac{\$500,000}{\$72,960}$$

GRM = 6.85

Suppose the same fourplex is projected to have $72,960 in $PSORI_{(a)}$ this year. If my purchase offer was accepted for $900,000, the GRM would be 12.34. Here the calculation depicts sale price is 12.34 times the $PSORI_{(a)}$.

$$GRM = \frac{\$900,000}{\$72,960}$$

GRM = 12.34

Please note: The $PSORI_{(a)}$ is the *same* ($72,960) when used to calculate the GRM. It does not take into account the OE or DS.

Let us recapitulate how the preceding figures enlighten:

Paramount Property–Purchase Offer–Analysis Form

(This form is in Appendix C, Appendix C-1)

———For Purchase Offer Accepted = $500,000———
Paramount Property–Purchase Offer–Analysis Form
_______*Property Address*_____
____

Unit Mix

Unit #	Rms	Baths	Mo. Rent	Yr. Rent
1	2	2	1,795	21,540
2	2	2	1,695	20,340
3	2	1	1,295	15,540
4	2	1	1,295	15,540
Laundry				
Other				
Total PSORI			**6,080**	**72,960**

Retirement Income & Expense Analysis

	Monthly	Yearly
TOTAL PSORI	6,080.00	72,960.00
Less Vacancy	00	00
GROSS PSORI	**6,080.00**	**72,960.00**
Less TOTAL OE	959.00	11,508.00
NORI	**5,121.00**	**61,452.00**
Less DS	1,798.65	21,583.80
CF	**3,322.35**	**39,868.20**

Operating Expenses

	Monthly	Yearly
Insurance	170.00	2,040.00
Water	00	00
Electric	00	00
Gas	00	00
Garbage	00	00
Fire Inspection Fee	9.00	108.00
County Health fee	00	00
Environmental Fee	00	00
Management	00	00
Repairs and Maint.	155.00	1,860.00
Property Tax	625.00	7,500.00
Total OE	**959.00**	**11,508.00**

CAP RATE

$CR = \frac{NORI_{(a)} \times 100}{V}$

$CR_{(\%)}$ desired = 6-12%

Actual Calculations

$CR = \frac{\$61{,}452 \times 100}{\$500{,}000}$

CR = 12.29%

CASH ON CASH RETURN

$CF = NORI_{(a)} - DS_{(a)}$

$COCR = \frac{CF \times 100}{AC}$

COCR desired = 10-20%

Actual Calculations

CF = \$61,452 - \$21,584

CF = \$39,868

$COCR = \frac{\$39{,}868 \times 100}{\$215{,}000}$

COCR = 18.54%

DEBT COVERAGE RATIO

$DCR = \frac{NORI_{(a)}}{DS_{(a)}}$

DCR 0.50 = Negative CF
DCR 1.00 = Break Even
DCR 2.00 = Strong CF

Actual Calculations

$DCR = \frac{\$61{,}452}{\$21{,}584}$

DCR = 2.85

GRM Calculations

$GRM = \frac{SP}{PSORI_{(a)}}$

GRM = (To compare similar listed properties ONLY)

Actual Calculations

$GRM = \frac{\$500{,}000}{\$72{,}960}$

GRM = 6.85

——For Purchase Offer Accepted = \$900,000——

Paramount Property–Purchase Offer–Analysis Form

Property Address

Unit Mix

Unit #	Rms	Baths	Mo. Rent	Yr. Rent
1	2	2	1,795	21,540
2	2	2	1,695	20,340
3	2	1	1,295	15,540
4	2	1	1,295	15,540
Laundry				
Other				
Total PSORI			**6,080**	**72,960**

Retirement Income & Expense Analysis

	Monthly	Yearly
TOTAL PSORI	6,080.00	72,960.00
Less Vacancy	00	00
Gross PSORI	**6,080.00**	**72,960.00**
Less TOTAL OE	1,364.00	16,368.00
NORI	**4,716.00**	**56,592.00**
Less DS	3,237.57	38,850.84
CF	**1,478.43**	**17,741.16**

Operating Expenses

	Monthly	Yearly
Insurance	200.00	2,400.00
Water	00	00
Electric	00	00
Gas	00	00
Garbage	00	00
Fire Inspection Fee	9.00	108.00
County Health fee	00	00
Environmental Fee	00	00
Management	00	00
Repairs and Maint.	155.00	1,860.00
Property Tax	1,000.00	12,000.00
Total OE	**1,364.00**	**16,368.00**

CAP RATE

$$CR = \frac{NORI_{(a)}}{V} \times 100$$

$CR_{(\%)}$ desired = 6-12%

Actual Calculations

$$CR = \frac{\$56,592}{\$900,000} \times 100$$

CR = 6.29%

CASH ON CASH RETURN

$$CF = NORI_{(a)} - DS_{(a)}$$

$$COCR = \frac{CF}{AC} \times 100$$

COCR desired = 10-20%

Actual Calculations

CF = \$56,592 - \$38,851

CF = \$17,741

$$COCR = \frac{\$17,741}{\$387,000} \times 100$$

COCR = 4.58%

DEBT COVERAGE RATIO

$$DCR = \frac{NORI_{(a)}}{DS_{(a)}}$$

DCR 0.50 = Negative CF
DCR 1.00 = Break Even
DCR 2.00 = Strong CF

Actual Calculations

$$DCR = \frac{\$56,592}{\$38,851}$$

DCR = 1.46 (approx)

GRM Calculations

$$GRM = \frac{SP}{PSORI_{(a)}}$$

GRM = (To compare similar listed properties ONLY)

Actual Calculations

$$GRM = \frac{\$900,000}{\$72,960}$$

GRM = 12.34

Summary of Paramount Property Purchase Offer Analysis

Purchase Offer Accepted for **$500,000**	Purchase Offer Accepted for **$900,000**
CR = 12.29% COCR = 18.54% DCR = 2.85 GRM = 6.85	CR = 6.29% COCR = 4.58% DCR = 1.46 GRM = 12.34
Best—CR Best—COCR Strong—CF GRM—Only to compare other properties for sale	Low—CR Very low—COCR Moderate—CF GRM—Only to compare other properties for sale

Now, I am indeed ready to make a tough call. That said, my gut feeling is strong and deep seated. And remember, I told you figures don't lie! Did you see the difference between these offers: One for $500,000 and the other for $900,000? I showed you the comparisons so that you can start thinking and doing some for yourself. Please choose some other offer, such as $600,000, $700,000, or $800,000. I have set-up the form in my Microsoft Excel spreadsheet and I recommend you do the same.

Note: If I use the same "Paramount Property Purchase Offer Analysis Form" to weigh in my *cash flow* for a specific property, I just change the name to "Paramount Property *Cash Flow* Analysis Form." You do not have to do CR, COCR, DCR and GRM.

To Buy or Not to Buy a Particular Retirement Property

As you will learn to appreciate, although these calculations provide rough investment evaluations, they are vital to making informed investment decisions from both the banker's and buyer's perspective. To me, it is the best, if not the only way to decide to buy or not to buy a retirement investment property. With these simple computations, you'll be a self-starter, well-informed cash-flow buyer. While super rich are essentially bargain hunters for cash flow, given their desires to pursue bigger nest eggs and to maintain their privileged class, in spite of this, their enormous opulence is what makes them happy as a king (or a queen).

Please note: The monthly retirement rental income figures are correct for this region in the city of South San Francisco, California. In fact, as of this publication, these figures are $400 below the fair-market rent, especially unit numbers three and four.

Unit #	**Rms**	**Baths**	**Mo. Rent**	**Yr. Rent**
1	2	2	1,795	21,540
2	2	2	1,695	20,340
3	2	1	1,295	15,540
4	2	1	1,295	15,540
Laundry				
Other				
TOTAL PSORI			**6,080**	**72,960**

Of course, the rental-market conditions keep changing, but the trend is generally upwards. Being super rich, if truth be told, involves the number crunching game in dollars and cents. Again, please crunch numbers for properties currently listed for sale today and become expert with these, and you'll see the magic of wealth building. The numbers game should not be mind numbing. Rather, it should make decision making transparent, to not to bite off more than you can chew. Or saving yourself from buying a lemon and be unsuccessful. How confident are you now? Extremely confident? Well, then you are extremely good. May God bless you in all your endeavors.

Buying decisions should also be based on:

Physical Location and Condition: Verification Process I

- Location, location, location
- Condition of the property
- The year it was built
- Who pays the utilities?
- How far is the property located from your residence?
- Above all, cash flow (CF) ** is the single most important criteria since we need to live on cash flow like the super rich.

**remember CF = NORI if you have a free-and-clear title.

Effective Due Diligence: Verification Process II

Get copies of the following items from the seller's agent:

- Current rent roll
- Rental agreement and/or leases
- Security deposits
- Property taxes
- Utility bills (if any)
- Service contracts (gardening)
- Management fees (if any)

- Income and expense statement (if any)
- Profit and loss statement (if any)

Verifying the seller's true costs in advance further guarantees our cash flow.

Note: Some buying tricks of the trade:

> Inspect all units with a camera and prepare a full report, audit all records, hire a professional inspector, renegotiate the terms if need be (request price reduction or ask for credit back for repairs), or finally offer "as is" with price reduction or credit at close of escrow (COE) (e.g., I ask for three to six months' rent credit at COE instead), or I may re-offer (an addendum) to get my original offer accepted.

Again, I look for a property that has all the utilities metered separately. I look for a townhouse property where the tenants pay all the expenses, including garbage, water, gas, and electric. For our nine-unit townhouse complex in the city of South San Francisco, California, the tenants pay all these expenses (garbage, water, gas, and electric). If the property is a good one, but the landlord pays some utilities, please do not get hung up over these, because they can always be changed after procuring the property. Rewiring of electricity and the repiping of water lines and gas lines with individual meters can be fine-tuned later, once you have attained the gold standard secret.

Please be sure to use your knowledge of the due diligence criteria to make the best buy. Foremost, we'll use the "Paramount Property–Purchase Offer–Analysis Form" to weigh in on the cash flow situation, and then we'll take it from there. It is the best of the best in its class for supporting cash flow transparency for decision making, and this will not only give us a clear numerical picture—perfect to recognize the COCR on our investment—but it will also give us the negotiating cutting-edge power for the price and terms should it not fit our needs. This is the super rich's way of negotiating the price with a clear view on COCR on a prospective retirement investment. The super rich have built tremendous wealth with all different types of properties, using calculations similar to the "Paramount Property–Purchase Offer–Analysis Form," and so can you. Basically, know the associated risk and maximize COCR on the retirement investment. Go ahead and make it a habit of analyzing many different investment properties for sale today and thereafter. So please gain the perfection by actually figuring it. I drive a hard bargain to get the purchase price to a fair-market value. Broker's pro forma figures may look to be encouraging but be careful all that glitters is not gold. And remember, no guess work here; think things through figures as you march on this journey to *rediscovering* and *redeeming* the American dream. The cash flow workable luck is with you now. Do you believe it?

Grand Finale Secret: Comes with My Signature Guarantee

By all means, select some listed properties in your region and do the preceding basic math formulae. As you have seen, cash flow predictions came from CR, COCR, DS ratio, and GRM, and those involved PSORI, OE, NORI, and DS. These special tricks-of-the-trade will help shine the spotlight on our cash flow purchase. Dwell upon looking to buy the best property and be willing to pay a fair market price for it. Using our down payment from our 401(k) or 403(b) or Thrift Savings Plan (TSP), federal government retirement account or, best yet, derived from personal savings, and/or borrowing a portion from a rich uncle to purchase the duplex, triplex, or fourplex should yield the best property money can buy. The idea behind these calculations is to buy the best and minimize associated risk. We are neither going to listen to the broker's pro forma, sugar-coated statistics, nor jump on an unfamiliar bandwagon to purchase a property without our "Paramount Property–Purchase Offer–Analysis Form" that clearly fits our needs and will calm our nerves. Again, we are here for the long haul, to buy our retirement property that will create generations and generations of wealth. In this case study, the figures reveal to us that if my purchase offer was accepted close to $500,000 it would have a strong cash flow. Yes, a good to best deal. Just think, in due course, if I pay off the loan and obtain a free-and-clear title (gold standard secret), I'll receive my NORI and that essentially will be my CF, NORI = CF. That's a good chunk of money. Inherently, I'm paying mortgage payments to myself! I am a mortgage bank! This is my grand inspiration! This is what I call the *Grand Finale Secret.* And this comes with my signature guarantee. I know buying a fourplex is easier said than done, but look at the bright side and have your heart set on the reward that comes with the title of the book: you create generations and generations of wealth. How rewarding! A most sweeping reward!

Please choose a plan of action yourself (one or all):

PLAN A I will purchase my first **Duplex** on ____________________ (Date of purchase)
PLAN B I will purchase my first **Triplex** on ____________________ (Date of purchase)
PLAN C I will purchase my first **Fourplex** on ____________________ (Date of purchase)

Great! Well done.

Inspirational Confidence Building

"Happiness is a positive cash flow."

—Fred Adler

"Cash flow is the roadway to fulfilling your dreams and wishes."

—Mahtab S. Ali

"If you really want something, you can figure out how to make it happen."

—Cher

"Every man thinks God is on his side. The rich and powerful know he is."

—Jean Anouilh

"It is never too late to be what you might have been."

—George Eliot

Chapter 5

The Property Management Procedure

LANDLORDING IS THE APEX OF THE PINNACLE

This is the apex of the pinnacle of wealth building, where we will learn to manage our money-making machine by means of a special apparatus called the property management procedure. To me, landlording is an art and a privilege; it allows me to become a small business owner without delay after signing the escrow papers. I am qualified to handle the situation. I know the ins and outs of landlordship. Unlike running a retail business, this rental business has a clear reputation for no onsite personnel presence. Periodic visits may be necessary to keep a watchful eye for certain maintenance work or really to appreciate the cash making-machine. Perhaps, less fortunate people (like rookie investors) never truly learn to see landlording as an ideal business. For some, this may be the greatest weakness in the quick start-up of such a business and an ultimate cause of failure. Education, along with proper tools of landlordship, is the solution. For example, use of superpower tools pave the pathway for running a serious business (subchapter detailed later). First, landlording skills are learned and then practiced, which of course makes it perfect. Perfection is only gained through practice and patience. Or better said: practice makes perfect, as a lot of us would say. Knowing patience is virtue; heeding landlord duties seriously and receiving no tenant complaints, is also one of the most inherent true virtues of this landlord responsibility. Respect them, because these are tenants who are giving us our retirement income, our lifestyle. Without them, I am going nowhere.

A great majority of people become landlords overnight by simply purchasing an already rented property. Becoming an instant landlord for some is a dubious venture and is probably not the best way to handle this business. While investors are blessed for buying a retirement money machine, most of them lack the training and accreditation to operate it, not realizing they own something that could potentially make any middle-class person rich. Most inexperienced investor landlords give up this goose that lays the golden eggs in a year or two because they find themselves ill-prepared to handle the day-to-day activities. I hear, "Oh, the property is for sale because the owner landlord can't handle the tenants' complaints and is giving up for good and wants to go into the retail business now." This landlord wants to shift the blaming game quickly and of course download the problem to a buyer. Or the landlord kept borrowing funds on the equity to the point where the property is running dry, no maintenance money left. I flag it as no preservation money. The uncouth landlord sucked so much sweet equity out of the property for his/her personal use that now he/she is a stricken slum-landlord and potentially ready to go belly-up. Note: This is a lesson to us all not to over borrow equity, and, in fact, it is quite in contrary to our gold standard secret rule.

The reality of the problem is that:

- The investor wanted to make a quick bang for the buck, because he/she heard or read about the easy road to wealth and was blessed with having enough hard-earned money (down payment) to buy the property.
- Was the investor a ready, willing, and able buyer? Able—Yes! Willing—Yes! Ready—(Are you ready?)—Fat chance! Clearly, the investor was neither equipped nor prepared (ready) to handle the activities of landlord duties.
- The investor never learned the proper lessons of property management procedure.

Most investors fail at this stage of managing their property effectively, and the worst part is they don't really understand why they really, really failed. They blame the tenants more than themselves. To me, they failed largely due to a lack of landlording education. I realize there is no practical course in colleges or universities covering property management procedures. Schools just offer the basic fundamentals or principles of real-estate classes, which typically do not include the day-to-day aspects of landlording. To me, it is a one-semester class, just to understand the nitty-gritty stuff of landlord-tenant relationships and the property preservation by reconditioning (rehab) and/or the maintenance process. Well, I learned the ropes slowly and perfected them during the time I became a landlord, not when I was a real-estate sales associate. Interestingly, as a sales associate, I never really thought of real estate as a small business venture and as means of passive stream of retirement income (PSORI), but today, they are my golden eggs. Again, this is the mark of this honored book and will convert PSORI into dollars and cents (money you can take to the bank), and this, when multiplied by the number of units and then by twelve, yields thousands of dollars of total annual

PSORI for just owning a fourplex. Even when I am sleeping, I am still earning my retirement money. That's the landlord's reward for landlording. I have tested and validated this procedure, and it is truly a never-ending money making machine that will create generations and generations of wealth through proper execution of landlordship duties. Recall our treasury of information on tenant responsibilities, which involve them paying for the utilities, including fines for breaking the ground rules including golden rules (superpower tools) spelled out in the addendum of the rental contract. Unlike large multi-unit properties, here tenants pay for almost all operating expenses (OE), including water, garbage, gas, and electric, and, above all, water-flow blockages are the tenant's responsibility when caused by their own carelessness and/or negligence.

What is the best-kept secret? The secret is who pays what. This should be planned in advance and clearly spelled out in the rental agreement and/or lease. Mind you, it does not stop here. It is the enforcement (ability to penalize for breaking the lease) of the terms of a rental agreement and/or lease that will bring us to this super rich's retirement income machine that we want. Don't we? This book contains the superpower tools to help us do that (sub-chapter detailed later). Thank God! And these superpower tools will give us the boost to stay on top, in line with the super rich's earning pattern, and we will not fail in creating generations and generations of wealth. These superpower tools are clearly marked in Appendix B and fully described in the subchapter "Nuts and Bolts of the Property Management," following the association resource. This is nothing new. These have always been the super rich's power dominance tools. It's about time to get a hold of it. It is about managing the property to profitability with the most effective yield. Please, please absorb this, and it will be programmed in your subconscious mind-set. My detailed explanations and procedures of the superpower tools will follow.

Association Resource

First and foremost, join a real-estate association that knows the ground rules of rental real estate in your region. In California, the best association that I know is Apartment Owners Association (AOA), which has its headquarters in Southern California. If you live in the State of California, I strongly recommend joining this association. Their Web site is: www.aoausa.com. Their annual fee is very reasonable and they provide an *Apartment Owners Association News* and *Buyers Guide Magazine* monthly to members and offer a number of good products and services, including credit checks, annual seminars, and classes throughout the year. Also some of these forms may be available free of charge from a broker or a sales associate in your region. Don't be afraid to ask them. They will be more than willing to help you. All they need is your telephone number and your address to do business. Keep in mind that you only pay them for their services by selling, not by buying. So I recommend you use them.

I use AOA's forms. I use their rental agreement and/or lease (ground rules) all the time and add my Appendix B-1: Addendum (golden rules) to the Rental Agreement and/or Lease. This allows me to add my own golden rules and regulations rather than just fill in the printed form. The primary reason for doing it this way (joining AOA) is that the real-estate laws are well followed in the state where I live, and then I can add my basic golden rules and regulations to it. A secondary advantage is that if the federal or state laws change, these associations are good at updating these forms. Basically, it eliminates the middle man, the lawyer who might overdo and mess things up. Therefore, the latest copy of my lease contains the required language. And certainly I can add clauses to suit my needs. Please, be proactive and make tenants pay for violating the rental agreement! Never forget that it is our business. Our real-estate business is run according to the law. By the written agreement, it's a lawful business. Don't forget this treasure. It's true, I can revise these golden rules and regulations in time or add new ones. First, I send them my new golden rules and regulations (by mail) with a return signature required and enforce it by monetary fine, if necessary. Details for collecting monetary fines are discussed in the succeeding pages.

For your information, here are the available forms for use by AOA Members:

- Application to Rent or Lease
- Deposit Receipt and Offer to Rent or Lease
- Rental Agreement and/or Lease
- Spanish Rental Agreement and/or Lease (Contrato De Alquilir Y/O Arrendamiento A Plazo)
- 30-Day Notice to Change Terms
- 3-Day Notice to Pay Rent or Move Out
  (Oakland) 3-Day Notice to Pay Rent or Move Out
  (Berkeley) 3-Day Notice to Pay Rent or Move Out
  (San Francisco) 3-Day Notice to
  Pay Rent or Move Out
- Spanish - Aviso De 3-Dias Para Pagar Alquiler O Mudarse
  3-Day Notice to Cure Violations
- Spanish - Aviso De 3-Dias Para Remediar Violacion A Su Contrato De Alquiler O Mudarse
- 0 Day Notice to Move Out
  60 Day Notice to Move Out
  90 Day Notice to Move Out
- Spanish - Aviso De 30/60-Dias Para Cambiar Los Terminos De Su
- Contrato De Alquiler O-Dias

- 60 Day Notice to Change Terms
- Receipt of Residents 30-Day Notice to Move Out
- House Rules
- Pool Rules
- Addendum to Rental Agreement for Additional Tenant
- Employment Contract
- Co-Signer Agreement
- Pet Agreement
- Right to Request Initial Move-out Inspection
- Notice of Intent to Enter
- Enter-Exit Checklist
- Security Deposit Refund
- Lead Based Paint Disclosure
- Lead EPA Booklet
- AB2330 Walk Through Process
- Notice to Rental or Employee Applicant (rejection notice)
- Hold Your Tenants Accountable! / AOA National Credit Alert Report
- Tenant Move-Out Report
- Notice of Belief of Abandonment
- Satellite Dish Addendum

- Receipt of Application Screening Fee
- NEW! Credit Check Service Agreement (CCSA) Tool Kit
- AOA National Credit Alert Report
- Annual Rent Control One-Time Charge

Rent Control

- 7-Day Notice to Move Out (Not for Apartment use. Intended for Hotels, Boarding House, and facilities only)

Others

- Tenant Account Record Reporting Form
- Credit Check Forms
- Northern California
- San Francisco Water Revenue Bond Passthrough Worksheet
- City of Oakland Notice to Tenants
- City of San Francisco Notice to Occupants
- Oakland - Just Cause for Eviction Ordinance (Measure Fee)

Nuts and Bolts of Property Management

Truly these are the nuts and bolts, the basics, the fundamentals, and the details of property management. Literally, nuts and bolts are much stronger than nails and screws. Nuts and bolts (e.g., anchor bolts) are used to hold together the main parts of our retirement money machine, the building.

Getting started in landlording is easy as well as rewarding because I present the nuts and bolts of the property management from A to Z. Unlike starting a new retail business from scratch, first, most of us will buy a property that is already rented—ready-set-go—therefore, the retirement money machine is already up and running. Now, all I need to do is meet my tenants in a friendly and professional manner. When I meet tenants for the first time, I deliver a written notice (Appendix B-1). It has almost the same information as is in Appendix B-2 and flagged as "Other Changes" added to it. This first letter is flagged as "Addendum to Notice of Changes in Terms of Tenancy." Remember to give twelve self-addressed stamped envelopes (SASE) to each tenant for mailing their rent checks, and also obtain both their current landline telephone number and cell phone number. There is no need to reinspect the property again since you inspected it during your due diligence period or a walk-through done prior to the close of escrow.

Now, let us learn to handle the paperwork we received from the seller and the seller's agent. Place all the letters, including the rental agreement and/or lease, in designated file folder for easy reference. Since we are talking about paperwork, it is a good time to learn the proper handling of the forms when one of the units becomes vacant. I may receive a telephone call from a tenant who wishes to relocate to another city or state for various reasons. I explain to the tenants that I need one month's written notice prior to them vacating the premises. Nearly everyone gives me a written notice to that effect. Some of them do not move out even after giving me one month's notice for various reasons. I stay calm because I know if the unit is vacant I will have to get the unit ready before renting it again anyway. I know it will be vacant for one month or less depending on how fast I get it ready and whether a prospective tenant is lined up.

For the type of property we are buying, I have created a prospective tenant card (PTC, Appendix D-1), of prospective tenants who want to move from the neighboring multi-unit property or from other places. It is my marketing tool, created from receiving telephone calls from prospective tenants wanting to rent. I always keep the PTC current and advise the prospective tenants to give me his/her new telephone number whenever they change it. Although, PTC of prospective tenants provides a roadmap of future tenants lined-up wanting to rent, it also gives a bigger picture of the need for business advancement, if needed. It's like the fish are coming to my fishing spot, where I put my fishing line in and I get my catch-of-the-day done quickly, so I can go to my home sweet home. In fact, this is my investment growth power if I want to purchase another fourplex—I have a bunch of tenants waiting in line to rent. Can you believe how powerful this PTC is? To me, it's a never losing business and with a strong growth potential. You make a move when the PTC is overwhelming. How great! A powerful surefire system in place to grow the business, if needed. This is what I call *PTC sure-fire investment growth secret.*

Now let us examine the proper procedure for handling tenant forms and the superpower tools next. Here, I have provided a checklist for quick reference.

Procedure for Handling Tenant Forms

1. Prospective tenant screening is important:
    - 1. Give application to tenant and review for completeness afterwards.
    - Do a credit check.
    - Call previous landlord for rent payment history.

- Verify employment.

2. *Never* give the key to tenant:
    - Before the whole lease agreement is signed.
    - Before a money order or cashier's check is received for down payment, including first and last month's rent.
    - Before a move-in inspection report is signed.
    - Before all repairs have been completed and the unit is ready to rent.
3. Fill out all forms at home with the help of a computer:
    - After filling out all of the forms, make photocopies for the tenant (the tenant copy, without tenant signature, is okay).
    - Keep originals for obtaining signatures (landlord copy).
    - Prepare twelve rental payment, self-addressed stamped envelopes (SASEs).
4. Arrange the forms for signature:
    - Rental agreement and/or lease
    - Addendum to the rental agreement and/or lease
    - House rules
    - Lead based paint disclosure form
    - Pamphlet: Protect Your Family from Lead in Your Home
    - Move-in, move-out inspection checklist

- Take a receipt booklet to document receipt of deposit and advance rent
- Twelve self-addressed stamped envelopes (SASEs) with full tenant address and your address to receive the rent check

5. Explain the forms in detail:
   - Do a walk-through and show all appliances, so on and so forth
   - Give the twelve SASEs to tenant
   - Give copies of all forms to tenant
   - Receive the deposit and one month advance rent, and leave receipt
   - Explain each page and obtain signature on originals
6. Keep originals in a special place and I suggest you make a file folder for easy reference.

Ways of Finding New Tenants (when the property is vacant)

- Offer a referral fee to existing tenants. Works great! (I offer $100 to $150.)
- Hold an open house.
- Place an ad in a local newspaper.
- Use of the Internet, blog, so on and so forth.
- Word of mouth.

- Post "For Rent" signs and post one sign in the window.
- Send direct-mail flyers to neighboring tenants.
- Your regional Housing Authority Agency may have a number of section 8 tenants.

Superpower Tools

As I indicated in the preceding pages, a premier piece of advice in this book is the apex of the pinnacle of the property management procedure and using the superpower tools to enforce the terms of the lease. This gives us the extra cutting-edge for wealth building and running a serious business. These superpower tools are in the appendices, namely Appendices B-1 through B-9. I name it as my "golden rules" because these rules provide protection to my golden eggs (PSORI). I will describe them in detail to ensure that they are used properly and strictly adhered to when needed during the property management procedure.

Superpower Tools (Golden Rules): Letters and Formats

Always charge tenants with monetary fine when they violate the rental agreements and/or lease. Use of the superpower tools is a must! When I started using the superpower tools, making tenants pay a penalty for violating the rental agreement, needless to say, it resulted in timely payment next time. In fact, every time. When I rehab a unit, the tenant knows that rent increase is inevitable, although, rent increase is certainly a function of the current marketplace. Appendix B-3, for example, is the Rent Increase Letter (format).

Appendix B-1:

An Addendum to Notice of Changes in the Terms of Tenancy
Its usage:
To change terms of the Rental Agreement and/or Lease:
—When the rental premises have been purchased
— (Includes Appendix B-2 information)

Appendix B-2:

An Addendum to the Rental Agreement and/or Lease
Its Usage:
To change terms of the Rental Agreement and/or Lease:
—Discount Program
—Drain Stoppages
—Payment of Rent
—Rent Payment Late Charge: After Fifth Day
—Rent Payment Late Charge: Beginning on the Tenth Day
—Garbage Disposal/Recycling Rules
—Rules and Regulations
—Other Rules
—Rent Check Bounce Policy
—Apartment Door—Lock and Key Policy

Appendix B-3:

Rent Increase Letter (format)
Its Usage:
—To increase rent after sixty days

Appendix B-4:

Rent Unpaid Beyond Grace Period (format)
Its Usage:
—To charge for rent that was unpaid beyond our five day grace period

Appendix B-5:

Partial Rent Payment Letter (format)
Its Usage:
—To charge for only partial payment of rent

Appendix B-6:

Drain Stoppages Fee Letter (format)
Its Usage:
—To charge a fee for cleaning drain stoppage

Appendix B-7:

No Rent Plus per Day Penalty Letter (format)
Its Usage:
—To charge for no rent received plus per day penalty

Appendix B-8:

No Utilities Payment Letter (format)
Its Usage:
—To charge for utilities unpaid

Appendix B-9:

Rent Check Bounce Letter (format)
Its Usage:
—To charge for rent check that had insufficient funds

Please make sure you have a #10 envelope to enclose the citation letter and a #9 envelope with unit number written on a self-addressed stamped envelope (SASE).

Very important, please note: these charges (monetary fines) are small amounts compared to the actual rent, but the message they carry is of prime importance.

Messages that Resonate from Our Superpower Tools (Golden Rules):

- That—you are a serious landlord, proper and just, and the tenants cannot beat around the bush. It further acts as a remainder for tenant responsibilities.
- That—you are running a serious business and things need to be paid or more fines/charges will accrue.
- That—it reminds tenants that payments are due on time.
- That—they can clearly see what contractual term they breached and talk about it among themselves.
- That—you have a well established discount program (incentive for on-time payment) payable as a reward check one month before Christmas (Appendix B-1).
- That—it can act to discourage a tenant from filing unnecessary complaints.
- That—above all, a late payment record (tenant violations) has been created about the tenant should you later need to evict them.

Self-Management Incentive

When I say it is ready to rent, it is ready to rent. I view my house as an example of my tenant's unit. When I moved from my previous house to my current house, I did some work to get it sparkling again. "Getting ready to rent" to me means that I would be willing to occupy the unit myself. Initially, I did the work myself in the evenings while keeping my day job. Now I have developed a list of contact personnel to hire to do the job. These are contractors, plumbers, handymen, and cleaners, a team ready to help me do the job fast. While leadership is a privilege and responsibility, a reliable workforce is the strength and endurance of our small business. That is, for a landlord to get a pat on the back, team spirit is the best business spirit to rally the troops in doing day-to-day self-management work. This is my team concept of the management help. Incidentally, this is my self-management incentive of collaboration (teamwork), and this is what I call *team concept of the management secret or collaboration secret.*

I have this list of contractors, plumbers, handymen, and cleaners from previous work they performed for me, and some are current tenants who are eager for extra employment. You just have to ask. I offer to purchase the materials and/or rent the equipment, but let a tenant do the work (e.g., painting, carpet cleaning). I pay my tenants to do a job, like repainting or touch-up painting to make it look as if all of it was freshly painted. (It is easy to do touch-up painting with the same brand and same color.) But sometimes it does need a fresh coat of paint all over. I know, I can't claim any work I do at my passive stream of retirement income (PSORI) property (IRS rule). If I hire a handyman to do the work, I prepare an IRS Form 1099 and just give it to the handyman. More often than not, a handyman performs the work, it is inexpensive labor compared to a licensed contractor. A handyman is my right-hand man. I tax claim expenses incurred for all the materials purchased for the job. For ease of reference, please keep all receipts in a separate dedicated file folder after logging them in an operating expenses log (Appendix A-3). Note: Appendix A-3 is Operating Expenses (OE) for a single property. I strongly advise my associates to manage a property yourself following this management team concept in mind, as discussed earlier. I do not have, nor do I recommend, hiring a property management company, except at the advanced stage of retirement. Next, we will learn how to properly record OEs for our tax account/tax preparer.

Logging Operating Expenses (OEs)

OEs are all expenses associated with running the rental property, except the debt service (mortgage payments).

OE Log Checklist:

Appendix A-3:

Operating Expenses Log

Its Usage:

—To document all maintenance/rehab expenses for a single property

Appendix A-4:

City and County Expenses Log

Its Usage:

—To document all fire department and health expenses and other city/county expenses (if any) for a single property.

Appendix A-5:

Capital Expenses Log

Its Usage:

—To document all capital expenses for a single property: new carpet, new blinds, new appliances, new roof, and new asphalt on the driveway, so on and so forth.

Appendix A-6:

Schedule E Log

Its Usage:

—To record Totals for Schedule E Tax Return for forwarding to our tax accountant/tax preparer.

Managing Tenants

Managing tenants is part and parcel of my daily routine. At this stage of my landlordship life, I have gained enough experience to be called a professional in managing tenants. Keep alive in your thought that our real-estate retirement investment is a small business and is in no way similar to retail marketing. Tenants are not retail products. They are people with feelings. They are the honey bees for my PSORI. My landlording work is rather easy compared to the work of a retail-shop owner who works long hours on a daily basis, sometimes with a teeny weeny profit to show for it. Owning and running a retail business is no laughing matter. I find myself having a lot of free time to do other things of interest. I provide my tenants a housing unit for a fee, and they in turn obey my general rules of the business game. The clear message here is that unlike retail marketing, I have all the time to effectively manage my tenants' needs and lots of remaining time left for me to do as I desire. Most of my ground rules are clearly spelled out in the rental agreement and/or lease, and the golden rules are in the addendum to the rental agreement and/or lease. Now, let's look at all-inclusive landlord-tenant responsibilities.

Maintenance/Preservation Guideline

A checklist for who does what:

1. Painting: I pick one brand of lone color paint for interior and exterior use. It is very easy to do touch-up painting by sticking to one brand, one color. For interiors, I like semi-gloss white. For exteriors, I like a two-tone color scheme: a dark color below and a lighter color above. For interiors, most of my tenants do the painting themselves or I hire a tenant neighbor to do it. For exteriors, I just have to rally the troops by hiring a crew of tenants every four to five years.

2. Cleaning a Vacant Unit: I have a dozen or more of my current tenants who are willing to clean a vacant unit in return for a small fee. I don't have a big problem with keeping things clean.
3. Carpet and Floor Covering: I have my tenants clean their own carpets by renting a carpet-cleaning machine from a local store. I offer to purchase the materials or rent the equipment. For new installation, I chose one good brand and color that is reasonable and looks good. I hire one carpet installer to do all my jobs.
4. Plumbing and Drain Stoppages: All my rental agreements and/or leases state clearly that water-flow blockages are tenants' responsibility when caused by their own carelessness and/or negligence. This includes clogged toilets, clogged showers, clogged bathroom sinks, clogged kitchen sinks, and clogged washing machine outlets.
5. HVAC: Heating, ventilation, and air conditioning are covered by tenants under utilities. My tenants pay for their own utilities. These HVACs don't need a lot of maintenance and don't often go out of service.
6. Appliances in the Unit: These are similar to HVACs, and they don't need a lot of maintenance and don't often go out of service. If they do, I have a big box store deliver and install a new appliance.
7. Yard Work and Grass Cutting: I hire a landscaping and grass-cutting handyman to do all my jobs. Some units don't need it at all, but some have concrete pavement and raised flower beds. Very little yard work is needed.
8. Snow Removal: I don't have a snow removal problem here in the city of South San Francisco, California, but folks in the high country of California and many

other states have this problem. Put it in writing, wherever possible, to have the tenants be solely responsible for snow removal.

9. Rubbish Removal: Put it in writing, wherever possible, to have the tenants be solely responsible for debris removal.
10. Smoke Detector: I know California state law requires smoke detectors in every bedroom, in the hallways outside the bedroom, at the top of the interior stairways, on each level in the dwelling that has two or more levels, and in the basement. I replace the batteries every year and record it in a simple smoke detector service log book. However, I also give a spare pack of batteries to the tenants to use in emergencies.

Guideline for Payment of Work Done by a Contractor:

- Get a signed written work contract before giving a 10 percent deposit check.
- Pay according to the payment schedule.
- Never pay the full amount until the job is fully completed.
- Verify with the tenant that the work was done satisfactorily (if you are not present at the work site).

Procedure for Recording Rental History and Monthly Rent Received:

The purpose of recording rent history and monthly rent received is not only for IRS reporting (Appendix A-1, Unit Rent Receivable Log), but for our own tracking as well (Appendix A-2, Unit Rental History Log). When did I last increase the rent for this unit? Every month I record the rent received info in Appendix A-1 (check number, date received, rent amount, and total year-to-date) and as I do so, I keep an eye on the Appendix A-2. I fill out the Appendix A-2 info only when I increase the rent. As you will appreciate, this appendix keeps me abreast of the history of rent. So again, keeping an eye on the Appendix A-2 (Unit Rental History Log) while filling out the Appendix A-1 (Unit Rent Receivable Log) will help you keep a better track record for a successful small business ownership.

Remember, we receive our rent check in the mail every time, all the time; that's how we communicate. Since I operate my business from the home office, I rent a private post office box (P. O. Box) to handle my business mail. And this may be an effective tool for folks who move often. Of course, you can use your street address if you choose to do so.

Let's now look at a logical way to record when our envelope is returned containing a rent check.

How to Document upon Opening the Envelope Containing a Rent Check

—On the left side of the same envelope put the (1) check number, (2) dollar amount (below it), and (3) the date of the check (below that). On the right side of the envelope, put the postmark date (sometimes the postmark date is very faint). See an example below:

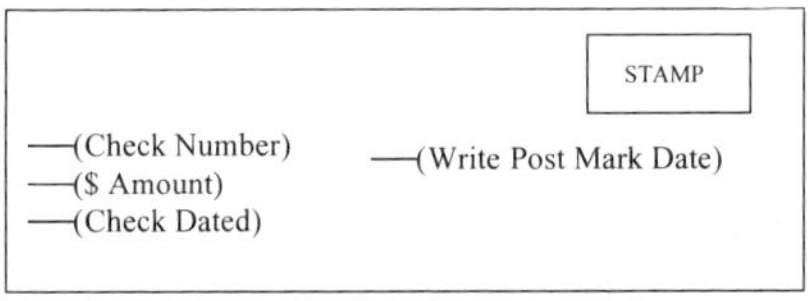

The reason of doing it this way:

(1) To quickly record check information before making a bank deposit.

(2) To correctly record dates (used in Superpower Tools).

(3) To later record this info in Appendix A-1 (Unit Rent Receivable Log).

(4) To create a permanent record if tenants ask questions.

(5) This serves as a quality assurance (QA) to double-check in case I did not correctly record the information in Appendix A-1 (Unit Rent Receivable Log).

A Checklist for Logging Tenant Rent Received

Appendix A-1:

Unit Rent Receivable Log
Its Usage:
—To accurately document monthly rent received from a tenant of a particular unit with running total (Total Year-To-Date). This should be placed on the right side of a binder. As I open the binder, I see Appendix A-1 (Unit Rent Receivable Log) on the right side and Appendix A-2 (Unit Rental History Log) on the left side.

Appendix A-2:

Unit Rental History Log
Its Usage:
—To accurately document the history of tenant rents from the amount that was initially charged up to the current rent. I update it whenever I increase the rent. This should be placed on the left side of a binder. Remember, as I open the binder, I see Appendix A-2 (Unit Rental History Log) on the left side and Appendix A-1 (Unit Rent Receivable Log) on the right side.

The appendices are primarily self-explanatory, although these will require some work to initially compose and set it up on the computer. Once it is set up and running, you may have to occasionally make a few changes and quickly print them. This is a good way to conduct a small landlording business. The super rich typically employ a property management company.

Always charge tenants with monetary fine when they violate the rental agreements and/or lease. To issue monetary fine, use the superpower tools formats which are in the appendices B-1 through B-9. You'll notice right above "Return this portion with your payment" there is a perforation mark, which the tenant is supposed to pull to separate it and mail that portion with the check (payment coupon). To do that, I use a paper perforator with a small rotary blade perforator attached to a cutting rail on a grid. This does a great job of creating a professional look. It looks just like the payment stub from a credit card company. Remember, we are used to receiving these from Visa/MasterCard/American Express companies, and it is no surprise to the tenants. Always charge tenants who violate the rental agreement and/or lease by using superpower tools. Whenever there is a need to write this up, I get paid, all the time. Well, sometimes it does take a telephone call to the tenant, and I receive a check and the lower return portion in the mail. So, it works. This is what I call *perforated payment coupon secret.*

Eviction Avoidance

Tenant eviction means removing the tenant (lessee) from the premises by way of legal processing and recovering possession of the property. The root cause of this is that the tenant is not complying with the terms of the lease agreement, the rental agreement and/or lease (ground rules), or other golden rules and regulations. Skipping rent payment appears to be the main cause. I am convinced in saying that most of my tenants conduct themselves in an admirable way and certainly pay their rent on time. Over my twenty-two years of being a landlord, I have had only two evictions initiated. One was settled by having the tenant pay all two months back rent. I did not lose any rent but spent $700 in court and attorney fees. In the case of the second eviction, the tenant moved out prior to the court date, and I lost one month's rent and did not pursue further in recovering it.

I find the superpower tools are the best for eviction avoidance. It is important to let the tenants know we are conducting a business, one with deadlines. The superpower tools can act to scare tenants into behaving properly, in an admirable way, thus avoiding eviction. If all else fails, we will be ready to quickly hand it over to a local real-estate eviction attorney with proper documentation.

Note: As a matter of fact, our superpower tools are razor sharp in discouraging the filing of lawsuits against us.

Inspirational Confidence Building

"Riches are chiefly good because they give us time."

—Charles Lamb

"Goals determine what you're going to be."

—Julius Erving

"The future is not a gift, it is an achievement."

—Harry Lauder

"Live life to the fullest, don't look back on the past, but look ahead to the future and hope tomorrow will be a better day than the past."

—Mahtab S. Ali

"Love and nurture your family, for they are your strength."

—Yasmin Ali

Chapter 6

Fears of Retirement Investments

OVERCOMING RETIREMENT INVESTMENT FEARS

We should overcome fear by remembering, "the only thing we have to fear is fear itself." This was very well expressed by President Franklin D. Roosevelt (FDR) in his first inaugural address in 1933, during the Great Depression. FDR indicated that it was only material things that Americans feared. I concur and believe that fear of material things can be overcome by application of a proven skill set (time-tested), which can and will establish, to a great extent, entrepreneur's fear endurance. My retirement money machine is, in fact, that proven skill set. As a result, this removes the associated risks and fears.

With strong determination, I constantly remind myself that fear of failure (fear of losing money) is perhaps the negative driving force in life. I use known calculated risk factors, thus avoiding the trap, for example, by using my "Paramount Property–Purchase Offer–Analysis Form" (Appendix C-1), which completely removes my retirement investment fear, and I am strongly banking on this idea. Consequently, taking written planned action with risk factors turns the fear off. I can visualize fear and then turn it off by knowing my property management procedure with superpower tools are first-rate risk removers, and therefore, first-class fear removers. If the risks are removed, fears are gone. This is what I call the *grand daddy fear remover secret.*

On the whole, acquiring retirement assets with simple formulas will do the desired trick. When we analyze it, it's the numbers, due diligence, and common sense that tell the true retirement investment story. These numbers ultimately end up in our bank account, once the task is accomplished, and that's one of the superexcellence fear remover reasons for pursuing this retirement course.

What's your biggest obstacle? Is it to face fear itself? How do you fight your fears? Are you ready to live a better life in your retirement years? Put priorities in your calendar. Find the team or a mentor who will help you turn your true passion into a career. For starters, those who have just started a day job, he could be a rich uncle (mentor)—talk to people about your passion and you'll be surprised how many are eager to help or just have a meaningful discussion. Learn from their mistakes and become the master of that passion. My endeavors are to surpass the current conventional wisdom of retiring then become the master retirement plan builder with the time-tested technique for the middle class. Once more, we actually begin to rediscover and redeem the American dream of ownership and self-control of our retirement life. Our retirement investment is slow but surefire.

Retirement Investment Is Slow but Surefire

Failures are a way to make you work twice as hard, because you have learned the lessons of patience and now you have the resilience. Let's say you bought a retail business, and in doing so you lost $100,000, and ultimately your business closed. You learned the lessons of your failure and now have the endurance to work twice as hard to recapture the lost $100,000 and then double it. The best way to recover the loss is to buy a fourplex and work toward attaining the gold standard secret. Now, go ahead and work twice as hard, and you'll certainly recover all your loss and more, and you'll be rolling in dough again. Ironically, I know a number of folks who have done completely the opposite of what I just told you. They bought a piece of real-estate property and built up a good amount of equity over time. But to my surprise, they sold the property and used the profit to start a retail business. You are right. They ran into financial woe. The business failed. They went dreadfully under. I mean totally out of business, and they came close to being homeless. They lived to regret their decision. They used all their personal credit cards in a failed attempt to rescue the dying business. They refused to relinquish control over the operations of the business. Again, how dreadful and painful an experience it must have been for them. You know what? They admitted their awful mistake of cashing in on the goose that laid the golden eggs. It was the biggest blunder. How detrimental. Down they went. This is a good lesson for all of us. No, I am not saying these folks should not have sold their property; I am saying these folks should have looked before they leaped, i.e., they should have sold and bought another bigger and better goose (proven time-tested skill set). Or on the other hand, they should have obtained a second loan only to finance their other project. Most folks make a lot of money in real-estate investment in time, either cash flow or equity. Time is a big factor here; time is of the essence. Remember, real-estate retirement investment is slow but surefire.

If you bought a piece of rental property and held it for fifteen years with absolutely no appreciation, but you worked hard and paid off the mortgage loan and obtained a free-and-clear title (gold standard secret), you would have a huge cash flow, because, in fact, your NORI is CF now. In reality, most folks do make a lot of money in real-estate retirement investment over time by CF and equity growth (by gradually paying off loan), but then they get greedy! Yes, greedy! They forget that it took them fifteen years to feed the goose to make it become fat and fluffy. Most investors fail by pursuing a brand-new skill set instead of sticking with a proven one (like ours). Here's the tricky part. They now want fifteen years of revenue in one year. You follow me. That's their greed, and down they fall! I believe that greed is Satan's best friend. Now you know the entire story. Please, please do not follow suit!

Please pause reading here to consider the point.

Please know that real estate investment is the best way to achieve a sustainable retirement income. And believe in yourself and overcome the hurdles, mitigate the risk. What do you do to mitigate risk? Do research and take an educated risk, meaning learn from the mistakes of others (like me). This is a powerful business skill set with proven results. I consider my mistakes learning experiences. I learned to handle pressure. My personal experiences show that most fears are easily overcome with wisdom. Make no mistake about it. When you act without using the "Paramount Property–Purchase Offer–Analysis Form," due diligence, and common sense, you run the risk of money woes ending up with a problem retirement income property. I mastered my personal skills, and my self-confidence slowly but surely drove my fears away. I learned that it gave me double the strength to gain the loss back, and the best thing is I did it. I work very hard to have my life filled with the thrill of success while avoiding the agony of woe. Through patience and resilience, I faced defeat and I turned it into the thrill of victory with the use of conscious mind-set and overriding subconscious mind-set. I confront obstacles and invest in myself and have full throttle control, like a licensed driver operating a motor vehicle. Well, I took the bigger risk and removed the risk from the equation. Therefore, a bigger reward is here for my associate, for just following my time-tested device.

Little Risks Have the Biggest Rewards

In this game plan, we will embark on a retirement wealth journey by taking and saying little risks have the biggest rewards. A good metaphor here is that when I am going on vacation to the Fiji Islands for example, it is so welcoming to me that I forget there are risks and fears associated with an airplane trip. My thoughts are only directed toward allure of travel and enjoying a sunny paradise in the archipelago. And a plea for merely thinking of the reward overrides my fear—just think of the mammoth reward of the gold standard secret.

Your retirement rewards should be based on the same principles, and, incidentally, this is the purpose of this thought-provoking book: to provide practical ideas that are as clear-cut, concise, transparent, viable, and straightforward, to move you swiftly on your life's journey full of goodness. Picture the teachings of this book in your mind and heart, gain the mastery of its compelling knowledge of wisdom, and surefire rewards will come to you.

I have learned that failure has a very short lifecycle in business. It is especially prevalent and most notorious in the initial stages of a business. A trophy in your work area is a reminder of the good times. During down times, it can certainly serve as an inspirational confidence building toward wealth building. Here again, the business of retirement innovation is a powerful commanding principle. I build resilience from my occasional failures. Recognize that once the foundation is built strong you are on your way. Most financial advisors would say: "The rule of thumb is to save six months' worth of income in case of a financial snag." Ours should be above and beyond the preceding guidance, more or less three years' income as an emergency cash cushion. Plan for the worst and hope for the best is my golden advice. Maintaining the speed and keeping a certain percent of reserve funds (emergency cash cushion) set aside is one of the secrets for creating generations and generations of wealth. Reserve funds should take care of our retirement needs during financial downturns. This is what I call the *emergency cash cushion secret.* To summarize, we should further recession-proof our plan by building a strong foundation: (1) Attaining the gold standard secret, (2) Implement emergency cash cushion secret, (3) Be in pursuit of having no debts, (4) LLC or Inc. your businesses. Through my failures, I am now a firm believer that the faster you fall, the faster you bounce back. Surround yourself with like-minded people. Take purposeful action. People said, "You couldn't do that!" but I went ahead, faced all odds, and borrowed money from my Thrift Savings Plan (TSP) federal government retirement account and used it to purchase my retirement money machines. I have done so repeatedly, until I have now reached the advanced stage of retirement. This is the best place to be. Later, you may join me. Please, believe in yourself. The sky is the limit.

Inspirational Confidence Building

"That some achieve great success is proof to all that others can achieve it as well."

—Abraham Lincoln

"The great use of life is to spend it for something that will outlast it."

—William James

"I hear and I forget, I see and I remember, I do and I understand."

—Chinese proverb

"Small opportunities are often the beginning of great enterprises."

—Demosthenes

"One of the biggest factors in success is the courage to undertake something."

—James A. Worsham

Chapter 7

Exit Strategy

WHY SELL THE GOOSE THAT LAYS THE GOLDEN EGGS

Do you know why some people exit by selling their lifeblood, the retirement money machine? Why would you sell the goose that lays the golden eggs for the golden years? The super rich won't do it. Why should we? Golden eggs are for a lifetime and more. This is the main idea behind creating generations and generations of wealth. In fact, create income from the wealth that is never-ending and also adding an emergency cash cushion (liquid cash in real-estate term) for you, and your loved ones, which basically is the road to super rich's institution.

We middle class want to start laying down the laws like the super rich. Pass this wealth to your loved ones, keep all the golden eggs, and never, never, never let them go. Our loved ones' future is too important to ignore. The renowned metaphor for this is a reserve battery or a reserve electrical power generator to give you light in times of turbulence in your life's journey as well as your loved ones. Clearly, it's a journey of a lifetime and more. Be fully cognizant of God, and God will be fully cognizant of you. In the same token, be fully cognizant of wealth, and the wealth will be fully cognizant of you. Take full control of your money and wealth by conscious mind-set in action every day, making it a ritual. If you can maneuver it by common sense and precedent, (e.g., this book's wisdom) you are in full control of your money and wealth—you are a rare individual! And incidentally, this is the super rich's dignitary monopoly. Most middle-class people sell a property after they made some capital gains, only to retire. This may be reinforced when they see retired parents sitting around the house doing nothing. People commonly equate retirement with inactivity. Many find their life savings rapidly depleting as inflation catches them from behind. If you sell the goose that lays the golden eggs in your golden years, then your subconscious mind-set was wrongly programmed when you were growing up. My subconscious mind-set says because my parents did not do such and such act, I fear I won't do it either. Creating and holding wealth and passing it on to the loved ones is the only solution. We can solve our behavioral problem by knowing more about subconscious mind-set and conscious mind-set.

Subconscious Mind-set and Conscious Mind-set

In a nutshell, these terms are defined as follows:

Subconscious Mind-set

Our subconscious mind-set consists of the sum total of our past experiences that are stored in our brain cells.

Conscious Mind-set

Things that we perceive by our senses of—sight, smell, sound, taste, and feeling—are controlled by our conscious mind-set at work.

Our memories, thoughts, dreams, emotions, behaviors, and our daily doings (habitual actions) are all controlled by the subconscious mind-set, of which we are by and large unaware; however, awareness of these are examples of the conscious mind-set at work. Our behavior is predominantly controlled by our subconscious mind-set, which determines our character. To fast forward, and fully enjoy and appreciate life, we need to weigh in on and understand our behavior and draw attention to our rational reason for doing things. We need to understand the underlying reasons, the way we do the things we do. Don't let your subconscious mind-set control you when you are in a distressed situation. Control yourself by being open minded through patience and perseverance. Control your negative thoughts and emotions. Believe in yourself, that there is a positive answer to a given dilemma and dwell on it. Be a savvy and resilient person in tackling a stressful situation. Being in control of the subconscious mind-set by knowing what your past experiences were like is the key to controlling them. This is what I call *controlling subconscious mind-set secret.*

Our subconscious mind-set controls negative emotions of the middle class when it comes to matters of wealth in the following ways:

- Since our parents were not landlords, we don't want this for ourselves.
- Since our parents never gave us wealth, why should we give wealth to our loves ones?
- We worked so hard in earning wealth; we want our loved ones to do the same.
- Our loved ones will have to learn to earn their own living.
- Our loved ones are better adults when they struggle to make a living.
- We will spoil our loved ones by giving them too much wealth.
- Our parents were broke, so are we.
- Our parents stayed on government welfare, and so will we.

I have entertained similar thoughts. Please understand that the super rich's subconscious mind-sets are completely opposite of the preceding subconscious mind-sets.

We can fight all our past thoughts and emotions by knowing and controlling them, and that is sufficient to change our subconscious mind-set.

When Should You Quit Your Day Job?

I should optimistically phrase this question as: when should you retire early from your day job? The optimal answer to that question should be: "I have attained the gold standard secret. I am ready to retire early now." I'll say, sensational! Super-duper! You're my associate. You should have a written plan of action and follow it and know how much cash flow to expect. This cash flow should be enough to cover all your associated living expenses and provide some savings for the rainy season (emergency cash cushion).

At the day job, the boss always dictates, "Do more with less." The voice in us should say, "Make more with less." Meaning, we will use our 401(k) or 403(b) or Thrift Savings Plan (TSP) federal government retirement plan to create generations and generations of wealth just in time. For me, this is an inspiration—food for thought—which makes me appreciate and respect my day job. These are the tricks of the trade that make my life valuable, and certainly purpose-driven. This certainly gives me the endurance to survive my day job dilemmas. It's time for us to grow up and take charge of our retirement futures and for our loved ones too in a slow, progressive, surefire way. This plan not only eliminates boredom in my day job, but it also keeps me firm on my two feet.

For those of you who just started your day job, stay in the loop of this journey of creating generations and generations of wealth. Please make a realistic plan of action for the next seven to fifteen year-period, to retire early as soon as you have accumulated enough funds in your retirement fund (401(k) or 403(b) or Thrift Savings Plan (TSP) federal government retirement fund or, best yet, derived from personal savings and/or borrowing a portion from a rich uncle) to apply as a down payment for the purchase of a duplex, triplex, or fourplex. Try to put the maximum amount into your retirement fund because later you'll use this as a down payment. That's exactly what I did during my starter years. I accumulated enough fund in my Thrift Savings Plan (TSP) federal government retirement account and used it again and again over a fifteen-year period. In the meantime, I located some income properties I wished to purchase.

For starters, you should visit a realtor to get an idea of current listings and prices. Choose some listings and do the math in chapter four to get a clear picture of cash flow transparency of your particular retirement investment. For now work toward accumulating the down payment toward purchasing your first property. After purchasing it, then, work at it until there is adequate cash flow. It has been repeatedly said, spend money to make money. Therefore, we will do exactly that. We are going to use our earnest 401(k) or 403(b) or Thrift Savings Plan (TSP) federal government retirement fund to strike it rich in cash flow and retire early. One of the major advantages of real estate as a fitting retirement tool is that it is a business that I can jump-start while keeping my regular day job. After purchasing the first property, you may do part-time work until the array of financial forces (cash flow) in you tell you it's time to retire early from your day job. The intent of it is to achieve financial freedom and stability, and that should create change in your retirement wealth income environment.

We are talking as little as one duplex to start with, a small start to drum up a small business. It is much, much better than buying stock, believe me, because you retain the money and ownership. To me, as little as a duplex is my own small bank. Next time, when you drive by a duplex, or a triplex, or a fourplex, think of it as somebody's bank, similar to one you could own. Through my teachings, you too can own that bank that will give you generations and generations of wealth via a passive stream of retirement income (PSORI).

I am a Millionaire Now!

Almost three decades ago, $100,000 was a lot of money for the middle class. Today one million dollars in cash at the bank is still holding its ground as a middle-class dream for self-sufficiency.

For me, the only way I can accomplish this is by business ownership, not by savings from my day job. Most big-business owners easily exceed the one million dollar mark. Remember, ownership of a fourplex is a business, a small business. And I say the one million dollar figure is attainable via this business enterprise. On the other hand, if you're willing to be especially frugal in saving on the road to hitting the million-dollar mark in cash via income from your day job alone, in the long run, it may require a lot of sacrifice which may be daunting and beyond your reach.

Not taking equity appreciation phenomena into account, it can be correctly said that, although I purchased a property worth one million dollars with some money down, my tenants and I, slowly surely in time, paid it off with a free-and-clear title (gold standard secret) while still working at the day job. *I am a millionaire now!* And this is what I call the *millionaire secret.* This is a surefire shot of becoming a millionaire. Additionally, if I set my mind to it and repeat the process again and again, what then I will become? A multi-millionaire! Just think of the cash this will leave in our bank account. Ooh la la! And this is what I call the *ooh la la cash flow secret.* That's exactly what I am trying to accomplish with a very strong conscious mind-set at the advanced stage of retirement.

Please pause reading here for a moment and think about the secrets you just learned.

Wealth Creation for Your Loved Ones

I have interviewed a number of middle-class Americans on the topic of wealth creation for their loved ones. Most middle-class Americans are egocentric (self-centered), giving little or no thought of leaving wealth to their loved ones. Perhaps their view of life is based on what their parents did to them. Although the middle class are more likely to be close to their children, they are unable to handle the subject of wealth creation. Over the years, I have observed numerous parent-child conversations. One example that I vividly recall took place at my in-laws' residence between a twelve-year-old boy and his forty-something mother. I was dismayed and startled to see the mother pointing a finger at the boy and saying in a rather strong tone of voice: "Look, Son! I always find you playing with this game gadget. And you still haven't finished your homework yet. Tomorrow is a school day. When are you going to start acting like a responsible adult?"

The son replied, "Mom, I am just a kid, like other kids my age."

The mother said rather abruptly, "Look, Son! We struggle so much for you. We give you everything, but when you reach adulthood, you're on your own. We're not going to give you anything after that point. By the way, we never got anything from our parents, so why should we give anything to you, Son! You have to work hard like we did all our lives. Listen! When you stand on your own two feet, then and only then, you'll find out! Do you understand?"

The son replied apologetically, "Mom, I'm sorry, I'll go home tonight and finish my school homework completely."

The conversation ended by the child's father calling from downstairs for the mother. Well, this is a classic example of a middle-class family not wanting to commit to providing for their loved ones, since they themselves received little or no financial support from the previous generations. At any rate, it does not sound right to me but this sort of thing happens all the time with the wealth deprived middle class and the matter persists subconsciously (subconscious mind-set). This subconscious mind-set hardship is deeply rooted and is frequently taken out on the next generation. I believe this process repeats itself among the middle class, and so wealth creation for your loved ones is not in the equation. This characteristic is peculiar to the middle class.

The middle-class person hardly explores the idea of wealth creation for their loved ones. For example, a stock share that I know could be purchased from www.oneshare.com for a newborn. You can directly buy shares of Fortune 500 companies including Walt Disney, Coca Cola, and Microsoft. So instead of taking a vacation and spending $5,000 to $10,000 for the trip, please put this money in the newborn's account. You can open the account using your name, and the newborn's name as the beneficiary. Remember, time is of the essence here. We want this to be a long-term investment. By age fifteen to twenty, the child will have accumulated a substantial sum of money.

Ironically, the reverse is true for the super rich. A number of studies show that the children of super-rich parents in turn provide assets, down payments, and investment opportunities to their children, mimicking their grandparents' behavior. Wealthy parents have wealthy children. Having wealthy parents may allow the children to undertake investment decisions like fourplex ownership. For the super rich, the fact that they own assets is enough to predict that their children will also. One of the best things a middle-class person can do is buy a fourplex for the adorable, adorable newborn. The rest is history. You and the newborn are certainly playing the super rich's monopoly game, and you'll be creating generations and generations of wealth for future loved ones.

Trusts (Revocable and Irrevocable Living Trusts), Wills, and Living Wills/Advance Health Care Directives

Trusts are very well-known entities used by the super rich for major estate transfer planning, benefits, and peace of mind. The super rich protect their personal assets by forming corporations: Inc. (Incorporated) or LLC (Limited Liability Company). Keep in mind; LLC and Inc. are not used to shield the business entities but rather to protect one's personal assets from malicious litigation. Remember, LLC and Inc. take the individual's name off the radar, so to speak. These are truly middle-class dilemmas, because the super rich have a well-established inheritance transfer asset protection system in place. To understand this situation, the central idea behind having trusts is to deter forced takeover by governments upon the principals' death by levying heavy taxes. These taxes include death tax, inheritance tax, property tax, capital gains tax, state tax, transfer tax, and so on and so forth. The IRS, state government, and the county tax collector all want us to avoid trusts and wills so that these agencies can collect more revenue from us, the middle class. Let's define these terms and learn how we can do the same as the super rich.

Trust

Trust is a written legal document (an agreement) whereby possession of property or money is transferred to another party upon certain conditions set forth by the givers (trustors or grantors).

We will learn that a trust is the best way to transfer possession of property to our loved ones. Trust is used by the super rich all of the time. A trust is a written legal document that is better than a will and is a complete substitute for a will. A trust is an enforceable document showing how a person wishes his or her property to be transferred without involvement by a probate court, whereas a will requires a probate court ruling. To make this a legal trust, it must involve three parties, namely: a trustor (grantor), a trustee, and a beneficiary, and it has to be recorded. The trustor and trustee have a living trust agreement; therefore revocable and irrevocable living trusts are born, and again, these are not subject to probate. A trust created while the trustor (grantor) is alive is a living trust, and the term is synonymous with the word revocable living trusts, which can be rescinded or changed. Since a living trust is a legal document, it should be prepared by a qualified attorney. Note: Be sure that you understand what you will be paying:

(1) How much the living trust will cost.
(2) How long the living trust will take to write.
(3) When will you be expected to pay your bill (all in writing).
(4) Who will record the living trust.

Let's now define some of the controlling terms in this subchapter.

A trustor is a person who provides a property and creates a trust.

A trustee can be a trustor (or cotrustees—my wife and I), a bank, or an institution that holds the title of the trust property and offers specially trained administrators to provide counseling and tax services.

Important note: most people name themselves as the trustee in charge of managing their trust assets until they become incompetent or pass away. My wife and I are both trustors and trustees (grantors) for our revocable living trust.

A beneficiary is a person or family group (loved ones) who are to be the recipients of benefits of the retirement income generated by the trust.

A revocable living trust is a trust that may be revised or revoked at any time by the trustor or trustors who created it.

An irrevocable living trust is a trust that may not be revised or terminated by the trustor or trustors once the agreement is signed.

Advantages of creating a living trust (revocable or irrevocable):

1. As trustees, we (my wife and I) gain legal right to manage and control the assets.
2. A living trust covers only those items explicitly spelled out in the trust (may be for a possession transfer of a single property only).
3. During the life of our trust, we earn our passive stream of retirement income (PSORI), and only after our death does the property possession transfer to our daughter (beneficiary).
4. Peace of mind: Upon our death, the property possession transfer is accomplished according to our wishes.
5. It allows us to revise beneficiaries (my daughter and grandchildren).
6. We can also appoint a fiduciary trustee (a bank or a licensed trust company) should we become incapacitated.
7. The cost of probate court possession transfer usually outruns transferring assets held in a living trust.
8. Get the original copy of the signed document after being recorded and keep it in a safe place. Give a copy to beneficiary(ies).

Advantages of Creating an Irrevocable Living Trust:

1. The trustor may not have to pay any income tax.
2. The possession transfer may not be subject to death taxes.

Will

Will is simply a written document that states to whom we wish to pass our assets (money and property) when we die. A holographic will is a completely handwritten will. For us in the middle class, there is a misconception that a will alone is a sufficient document to avoid probate court in the transfer possession of property. A will still requires a laborious court-supervised process (probate court) to transfer possession of an asset to a beneficiary listed in a will, whereas a trust does not. A will may require one or two witnesses. People write wills and over the years often change the beneficiaries' names; therefore, it is the last will that stands in a probate court. Nobody can change a will except the person writing the will, not even the attorney-in-fact (power of attorney).

A will for the middle class is a way to get us in trouble when transferring assets. (Note: a young married couple without significant assets or children may not benefit from having a living trust.) The super rich's loved ones get all the inherited wealth and stay rich without paying an arm and a leg, whereas sometimes the middle class wealth simply does not go to them. It goes to the government, the state government. It's no surprise to me, they even call it escheat. The state government is an: es = estate + cheat = escheat. It is said that the property is suffering from lack of a will or a trust, and, therefore, it is escheated by the state government.

Escheat is defined as the reversion of a property back to the state government in the event that the property owner dies without leaving a will or a trust (and having no legal heirs).

Learning from the preceding discussion, we will deliberately treasure our assets like the super rich and protect them from malicious takeover by the government or rulings by the probate courts. The major estate transfer planning benefit is to ensure our loved ones (beneficiaries) receive the property according to our wishes and certainly with peace of mind. Therefore, a living trust creation is the key and is the most important part of our estate transfer planning. If I create a living trust (revocable or irrevocable), I don't need a will. In a trust situation, the titles to all our properties are then held as trust.

Living Will/Advance Health Care Directives

A living will is also known as an advanced health care directive.

A living will is simply a written document that clearly states our specific decision to caregivers, in advance, whether or not we want to be kept on artificial life support. Due to our incapacity, we may not be able to give informed consent; therefore, this assures our wishes are followed, rather than leaving the decision to loved ones. A living will document can be created and flagged as a living will with a certain date of declaration that may be made with two witnessed signatures.

Inspirational Confidence Building

"Wisdom is the most important part of happiness."

—Sophocles

"There are two things to aim at in life: first, to get what you want, and after that to enjoy it."

—Logan P. Smith

"People make their own luck."

—David Liederman

"Success covers a multitude of blunders."

—George Bernard Shaw

"He that can have patience can have what he will."

—Benjamin Franklin

Chapter 8

Enjoying the Retirement Responsibility

I deeply feel and firmly believe that after attaining the gold standard secret of this book, you should pride yourself on the best ways of enjoying the retirement life: being happy (life, liberty, and the pursuit of happiness), being self-content, taking the responsibility, and appreciating the benefits.

"Life, Liberty, and the Pursuit of Happiness"

As you will discover, this book attempts to reawaken and redeem the secret of our nation's founders' message contained in the phrase "In God we trust." Our Creator, our God, has granted certain "unalienable rights" to Americans. "Life, liberty, and the pursuit of happiness" is one of the renowned expressions in the United States Declaration of Independence of the thirteen colonies, which had been unanimously agreed to that principle as set forth in the Bill of Rights.

The nation's founders completed their mission by writing the last fabulous grand sentence: "And for the support of this Declaration, with a firm reliance on the protection of divine Providence, we mutually pledge to each other our Lives, our Fortunes and our sacred Honor."

This book is greatly inspired by the same principle.

"We" (the reader and the author) will mutually pledge to each other to redeem our lives the American way—to truthfully enlighten and seek prosperity and enjoy retirement life.

Our Fortunes (to create Generations and Generations of Wealth)

And our sacred Honor (a blessed admiration):

- To accomplish this book's secret teachings.
- To change our subconscious mind-sets.
- To retire early and be rich.
- To create wealth for our loved ones.

I see the intent of the founders of this nation as apparent and precise, truthful and compelling, with clarity of purpose, to grant us certain freedom, to uniformly vow to one another for mutual survival in this world, and to seek prosperity and enjoy life, including retirement life. Specifically, the book cover features an image of a family tree made out of symbols of money. This image depicts one of the ways of making money via the book's wisdom that will last for generations and generations to come, and this is what our forefathers left behind. Thirteen branches emphasize the strength of the original thirteen-state union that stood on a solid foundation naming the United States of America.

The pyramid and the seal at the back of one dollar bill is very symbolic. It represents two sides of our great seal of the United States. Side one has the symbol of the pyramid, and the flip side represents the great seal itself. Side one, I believe the "eye" (small eye pyramid) symbolizes oneness of God overseeing and blessing the big pyramid below having thirteen steps (thirteen-state union or providence). I believe the term "protection of divine providence" further affirms that this nation shall not perish from the earth. And the secret catchphrase recapitulates the inscription on the back of all the U. S. bills as: "In God We Trust" for prosperity. We Americans need to redeem this land of unique opportunity as sought by our forefathers. All Americans are created by God to be equal and just—an American statement of belief, an American creed—a perfect union. The United States of America is blessed with having unity under one God, a just and unified people not engaged in tribal warfare. This is a promised land held in reserve by our forefathers, where there is life, liberty and justice for all, including foreigners. Our forefathers seriously heeded "Life, Liberty, and the Pursuit of Happiness," and they crafted and created a road map to pursue happiness and wealth. It gives us the reassurance of living a good, healthy, and wealthy retirement lifestyle without depletion of funds. Our "sacred honor" is to get divine approval to change our subconscious mind-sets and for our loved ones to strive to be rich and stay rich. Regard life and property as a sacred trust. It also gives us reassurance of individual obligation to one another—to seek out prosperity—via life, liberty, and the pursuit of happiness.

Pursuit of Happiness

Now I want to draw your attention to the pursuit of happiness, as a right of a people to pursue their happiness as they desire while not harming others. Our nation's founders were certainly inspired by having the final building block, pursuit of happiness, in the Declaration of Independence. They conceived the idea that having natural rights as "free men" signified happiness. Pursuit of happiness is in essence our right to be enjoying the retirement responsibility (title of this chapter) of our small business (i.e., owning a duplex, triplex, or a fourplex). In the context of this book, does having a duplex, triplex, or a fourplex (retirement money machine) buy us happiness? I am a firm believer that possessing and managing wealth for prosperity can bring us happiness. Being in pursuit of happiness in the face of fear is the key. Happiness is a God-given privilege, not a right, and its pursuit is essential for survival. Although happiness is a relative matter, it can be hilarious too. It has been said that laughter is the best medicine (but please don't laugh like Satan). Additionally, I believe that personal financial freedom is an essential element to the pursuit of happiness. In fact, this beloved book's wisdom is in the pursuit of happiness. If you seriously, genuinely, honestly, and truthfully follow this book's teachings, it will lead you to the pursuit of happiness. It is the ways and means to the end. Halleluiah, Alham-du-lilla, Boruch Hashem, Jai Bhagwan/Namaste, Salamat Sa Diyos, Alabar a Dios, Gan xie shen/Gum ger suen (Praise the God, or all praise belongs to God, or blessed be God).

Appreciating the Responsibility

Happiness is the recipe to appreciating responsibility. I have dedicated my career to helping people create and preserve wealth through innovation and also to hold it for generations and generations to come. I appreciate and respect my responsibility. I make a supreme effort in planning for my lifestyle and look forward to fulfillment in my retirement years. Most people don't know that our time-tested device comes with lots of extra bells and whistles, including:

- A planned incentive to work hard at our day job and save for a down payment.
- A motivation to save and pay off the mortgage (free-and-clear title).
- Knowing that revenue for retirement is entirely within our control.
- Controlling conscious and subconscious mind-sets to create generations and generations of wealth for us and our loved ones.

That said, I have decided to work above and beyond for my retirement's sake. These features clearly demonstrate tips and tricks that will bring a big win in our life. I truly enjoy life, working, vacation, dinner table conversations, and so on and so forth, knowing that my retirement plan is in order. I have to think big, but I may start small, and it may be the only way to start for some of us. Big ideas should inspire us to the point where we start enjoying life as if we've already made it. Starting small gives me the opportunity to handle the situation, meaning, start with the purchase of a duplex and go from there. But I still say go for the big one: the fourplex, if you can clear the pathway to reaching it.

With a well-planned conscious mind-set, work hard to achieve it. I know from my experiences that this came to me with substantial performance expectations. If many others have done it successfully with this proven skill set including me for establishing a reliable retirement income, so can you. This is what I call the *time-tested device secret*. It's true! Take it from me!

Understand that we live in a natural world, but some super rich citizens have made it a deceptive world surrounded by commercial ads that deceive us. We are victims of daily bombardments of media malaise: commercial ads, TV ads, radio ads, and newspaper ads that attempt to brainwash us, persuade us, program us, and condition us (e.g., to be compulsive consumers of junk food). It appears that these commercial ads rule our lives. Obesity is a growing problem. Kids get hooked on technological marvels, including the Internet, cell phones, text messaging, and protracted cell phone conversations with no meaningful benefit. Certainly, we have more electronic gadgets in our homes, and we are carrying more of them in our ears, cars, pockets, and purses. But are we happier than the previous generation?

Why does happiness matter to us? It appears that we may not be happier than the previous generation, but I believe we can turn this around. Again, happiness is appreciating the retirement responsibility. We will attain what our forefathers sought but never grasped. Please be clear in this thought. We will innovate to change our subconscious mind-sets to lead an intentionally purpose-driven in pursuit of happiness. Americans are the best innovators. We can create a self-controlled power by intentionally ignoring negative vibes. We can also make our loved ones gain prosperity like the super rich. We will certainly do a great service to this country and to the world, and to the Almighty, our God, in appreciating the responsibility and redeeming the American treasure.

Fulfilling the Pleasures of Divine Inspiration and Happiness

Please elevate yourself by owning a fourplex, and diligently and patiently working to pay off the debt while being employed at your day job, and also patiently praying for deliverance of free and clear title to attain the gold standard secret. This book not only preaches retirement innovation for the middle class but also resurgence of good old faith in America. Appreciate that signs of God's blessings are love and mercy and if we in turn show love and mercy to the people of the world, including family, neighbors, and people of different faith, then surely God sends his divine blessings on us through love and mercy. We serve God by serving humanity.

Our Lord give us:

- What is the best in this world.
- What is the best in the next world.
- Salvation from the torment of the hellfire.

What is the best in this world?

It is to be divinely blessed by God with:

1. Wealth
2. Knowledge
3. Good health and long life
4. Spouse and loved ones

Fulfilling the Pleasures of Divine Inspiration

Hurt no one, so that no one may hurt us. I say this is God's divine power to bring peace and harmony in our souls. I know my inner heart's feelings are attached to God's divine superpower command control. God knows what is hidden in my heart. Any good that flows through my heart into my mind is truly a divine message, a divine thought, and will have a divine reflection. I understand that I need courage and purpose to be in pursuit of happiness in this world intentionally, and strive for it intentionally, even if my brain at a subconscious mind-set stored negative memories from my childhood days. Glorification of God is one of the true essences of progress and enjoyment in life. May God's splendor be glorified.

Spiritually, what I want in this world is God's divine blessings and with good fortune—generations and generations of wealth. We all eat food to be alive, similarly, performing daily prayers are acts of providing food for the soul. And purification of one's soul is achieved by being pious with heartfelt prayers. In fact, seeking God's divine help in prayers is pursuit of happiness of the soul itself, a true inner glow of happiness. Be God conscious through piety. Prayer restores connection with God and is the true inner essence of worshiping God. This is what I call *fulfilling the pleasures of divine inspiration secret*, through which my inspiration for God lives on. I am certainly inspired by the fulfillment of my prophesies. Still, I am extremely afraid of the wrath of God (tests or trials); therefore, I shall prepare for it (prayers, alms, patience, humbleness, healthy eating habits, including emergency cash cushion) as reserve during adversity. Every morning after I wake up from sleep, I thank God for giving me life.

God willing, I am committed to uplifting my daughter's lifestyle by building a strong retirement plan with PSORI and developing—an elegant retirement heritage (at an early age). This is great! Since this is a parallel wish to my goal (this book's wisdom), it inspires me and makes me tick. I trust my intuition. Also, I am surely getting ready, in time, to advise my grandchildren how to handle their wealth and lifestyle. I can create a happy environment for myself and others. I work for it, and look forward to enjoying it. I want my legacy to reflex as prosperous, and radiant as a bride.

Fulfilling the Pleasures of Divine Happiness

To me, attaining the gold standard secret is the best for sustained success. I am asking God for this worldly wealth, and I want to purify my wealth through alms (a philanthropic pledge, giving to the poor) so that I may receive the best in this world (God's blessing) and the next world. If I give alms to the poor, in God's eyes, I've got a heart of gold. Giving alms to the poor is a positive consequence of having extra wealth for sharing. I believe that sharing of wealth, especially with a poor person, is one of the very essences of receiving God's blessing. This is what I call *fulfilling the pleasures of divine happiness secret.* Just think what a fabulous job our wealth can do by making the poor happy: giving alms. Upon receiving the alms, the poor will certainly thank me for the token of appreciation and will pray to God for blessing my wealth. You see, in reality, I am the beggar for the poor's blessing upon me. In giving alms, I am assured in getting God's blessings, purification of my wealth (protects it from misfortunes), as well as purification of my heart from all forms of greed and selfishness, and the multiplication of good deeds. I believe it can be correctly said that the super rich and the rich are at the mercy of the poor's blessing to purify their wealth.

God wants us to perform regular prayers and give alms to the poor. Who is God talking to? I believe to the super rich and the rich. If I am rich, I'll honor God for that and certainly commit to being humble. The notion that God is closer to the poor is a misnomer. I don't look down at the poor as poor but with a sense of humbleness and goodwill. I believe that humbleness and goodwill are divine virtues. Conversely, if I am poor, it is understandable that God will not ask me to give alms, but it is a dismal position to be in. Don't the poor want to be rich? Don't the poor ask God to make them rich? God certainly does not want us to be unhappy in this world. The poor should work twice as hard to seek God's divine blessing to be rich. Ask God to make you rich so that you in turn can also give alms, just as the super rich and rich do to purify their wealth and perform regular prayers to purify your soul.

I believe that true faith in God can help you resolve wealth, personal, and family challenges. And I believe the family that prays together stays together. Be God conscious all the time and admire his creations at least once a day. In conclusion, we desperately need God's divine blessings on us while on earth. Unquestionably, this book's wisdom and strong advice supports this undertaking. In fact, obedience and observance to God's divine laws in daily practice in this world are the proper pathway to this journey back to God for the next world, because none of us know when our time is up. God bless.

Inspirational Confidence Building

"The greatest tragedy of life is not unanswered prayer, but unoffered prayer."

—F. B. Meyer

"The deepest wishes of the heart find expression in secret prayer."

—George E. Rees

"Prayer time must be kept up as duly as meal time."

—Matthew Henry

"The one thing worth living for is to keep one's soul pure."

—Marcus Aurelius

"No prayers can be heard which do not come from a forgiving heart."

—J. C. Ryle

Chapter 9

Be Organized in Life!

BEING WELL ORGANIZED

Organization is the key to having a comfortable, convenient, and balanced lifestyle. Through trial and error, and of course through innovation and inspirational confidence building, I learned that organization is of the very essences that motivates me to accomplish daily tasks, giving me the energy to go on. Organization helps me to uncover what I will be doing the first thing tomorrow and the time frame in which to complete it. In today's world, we have repeated this phrase many times: "We have so much to do and so little time to do it," such as meeting time frames and deadlines. Being well organized in life certainly gives me the stamina and willpower to succeed; since punctuality is the soul of business.

Power of Spontaneous Revamping

I actually don't have to do tomorrow's work today, but just before I end the day's work, I always leave myself some written directive that will quickly remind me where I left off. The next day upon gazing at the directive, my eye tells my brain to quickly reestablish the thought process. This is what I call the *spontaneous revamping memory secret* to inspire me to start work again. This power of spontaneous revamping memory power is very common among kids. They leave all their toys behind "as is," particularly when the mother or father is calling it a day. The next day the kid approaches the play site and says, "Oh that's where I left it." The kid is inspired. I believe the kid has already done some portion of the day's work and can quickly commence the task. Well, we adults could follow this example. Perhaps, it's natural standard, a God-given inspiration. To me, it is a prelude to accomplish other tasks, such as receiving retirement rental income from tenants and logging them in the file folder at the end of each month, and mailing out those penalty notices if needed (superpower tools). Anyway, let's use this inspiration technique at the very beginning of a day's job for proper direction.

The prerequisite for starting any task is to remember to reward yourself when you complete it. It's an inner inspiration (conscious mind-set reward) to accomplish the task. In this day and age, we have numerous tasks to accomplish. I have mastered the art of the initiation phase by which I mean just doing something small in line with something big. Approach a big task in small steps. Once the work is done to my satisfaction or truly finished, I reward myself. Little rewards for my body are wholehearted rewards for my mind. For example, a tea or coffee break or a mini-rest reward (or something as big as a vacation for attaining the gold standard secret!).

Now that you have learned how to be a good landlord, I know you'll work hard in getting rent money collected on time and levying fines on tenants who are late in making their payments. And please do not give your hard-earned money back to the credit card companies or mortgage companies in the form of late payments.

I am careful to making mortgage payments on time. I keep a zero credit card balance and pay no interest. I charge it, and as soon as the bill arrives, I totally pay it off. Also, I made a promise to myself that I don't sleep until I have opened the day's mail and disposed of it.

Business of Bookkeeping Secret

To avoid being overwhelmed with work, I try to do chores of landlordship on a daily basis. Right after purchase of the retirement property, bookkeeping (record keeping) provides the foundation to succeed effectively and timely as a retirement investor/landlord. Proper business of bookkeeping eliminates tedious tasks of shuffling paperwork here and there, and by all means, is the key for being well organized in our small business. This is what I call the *business bookkeeping secret*. I tell you, bookkeeping of day-to-day business is of utmost importance in answering questions such as:

- What is my current cash flow?
- Should I purchase another retirement property, or is this cash flow enough for my retirement income?
- Am I ready to purchase a retirement property for my loved ones?
- Is my IRS record keeping updated?

I keep receipts for everything I buy and record them in an organized manner like the operating expenses (OE) record keeping. Supplies used toward running and maintaining this small real-estate ownership business are tax deductible, including office supplies.

My Wellness Home Sweet Home

> The state of being in good health is wellness. And the precursor for good health is being in good spirits. Having a healthy environment in the home can certainly improve our quality of life.

It seems as though we just can't escape from the stresses or frustrations of our daily life, but somehow we manage to survive the ordeal. Perhaps fear of failure may be the biggest driving force. We are swamped: the pressure of being late to work; taking care of loved ones, the spouse, and the elderly parents. There is hardly time available for us to rest and relax in order to rejuvenate. We have a lot on our plates, we crunch the time, and somehow we still hang in there.

Sadly, for some of us, stress relief takes the awful form of indulging in overeating. For example, most chocolate connoisseurs don't realize that they are over-indulging in being such a sweet tooth. Being overweight can lead to diabetes and other serious diseases. Some of us consume massive amounts of ineffective herbal medicine/supplements at an exorbitant price, each day pleading for good health. Some of us sit and watch TV too much and have difficulty getting enough sleep.

We need a wellness innovation to be in tip-top shape. It's time for a wellness change and optimism, a change we can gain through a passion for our wellness home sweet home. We need a lifestyle that promotes an ideal wellness. I want to rediscover and redeem an American strong wellness home sweet home again, just as I did in grabbing the golden opportunity for my retirement innovation. Our lifestyles can be improved by having a quality wellness home sweet home. My family's good health is all dependent on practicing strong wellness plans. What do we do? Just a simple walk every day, less than a mile in length, can take care of our daily cardiovascular exercise needs and will make you feel like a million dollars. Do not be a couch potato; instead, work out, go out, or just walk. The key is planning: drawing up a written action plan and adhering to it.

List for an ideal wellness home:

- Pleasant home sweet home environment
- Nutrition and diet allowances
- Fitness programs
- Family communication
- Rest and relaxation

My Balanced Way of Lifestyle

Some surefire habits for a healthy lifestyle are:

- Developing healthy eating habits. For example, please do not watch TV while eating. When you concentrate on exciting scenes, you easily forget the amount of food you are consuming. This is habit forming. It is an unhealthy eating habit. Well, once in a blue moon it won't hurt.
- Drinking enough water. I adopt a balanced approach to diet, including drinking enough water every day. Our kidneys need water to flush out toxins from our system. I can safely say, water is a natural appetite suppressant. Try this, drink one half glass of water prior to eating a meal.
- Getting adequate sleep. Sleep is a healing medicine for the tired mind and body.

- Doing regular physical exercise. This is the body's daily dose of natural medicine. It burns calories, improves blood circulation, reduces excess body weight, tones muscle, and above all, it is just what the doctor ordered!

More Golden Nuggets

My Wonders of Living Summary:

- Our home is a rest ground, where not only our hearts and minds are comforted but also revitalized with strength and courage.
- Our home is a nest ground, where not only parental love and spousal love are respected and cherished with dignity but are also respected and nurtured with dignity.
- Our home is an institution, where not only do we learn how to create generations and generations of wealth but also cleanse our souls.
- Our home is a vacation home, where not only do we plan for a day's tour but also satisfy our requests and needs for the day.
- Our home is a theater, where not only the drama of our family life is played out but also true stories of passion for love and joy of family values are molded in our subconscious mind-sets.
- Above all, our home is a pleasant home sweet home, where not only are the virtues of beauty and truth

learned, but also the pursuit of happiness is practiced, and God's love and mercy are received and thanked.

My administrative wisdom for a better business lifestyle:

- Signed Copy: I always insist on obtaining a copy of any document that I sign at the time it is signed.
- File Folder: I always create a separate file folder for an account for easy reference.
- Plan Ahead: I always write my next day's plan and carry it with me, and monthly and yearly plans are posted on a wall calendar.
- Be on Time: I always try to arrive fifteen to twenty minutes ahead of the stated schedule.
- Do Your Homework: I always prepare myself before the start of a task.
- Clean the Mess: Once a week, I make a point to clean the mess on my office table.
- Quality Assurance: Above all, I always do a Quality Assurance (QA) check on my work to ensure it is doable and all mistakes have been removed.

Inspirational Confidence Building

"Success is the sum of small efforts, repeated day in and day out."

—Robert Collier

"Happiness, I have discovered, is nearly always a rebound from hard work."

—David Grayson

"Happiness is a conscious choice, not an automatic response."

—Mildred Barthel

"Family life is the source of the greatest human happiness."

—Robert J. Havighurst

"Treat your children with kindness for they are your flowers for the future."

—Yasmin Ali

Chapter 10

Graduation and the Advanced Stage of Retirement

GRADUATION TIME

Way to go! You've done the required reading and earned your graduation accreditation. You deserve a pat on the back. You are now my associate. Today it's time for you to enjoy, and tomorrow you'll embark on this hugely ambitious fruit-bearing journey and test your skills in the real world, or you may simply pledge yourself if you are just starting your day job. Although my time-tested device is congratulatory, given my expertise and passion for sharing the wisdom, I hope it'll open a new door for the all-American middle class craving to follow suit for this retirement innovation. So please be the first in line.

Please recognize that it is one of the most attainable approaches to wealth creation and being in self-control, once and for all, is faithfully crafted for you, along with a heart of gold prayer (author's final words). So please plan, plan, plan, and stick to it.

Needless to say, my associate, this should become our elegant retirement heritage. Please embrace it and uphold the author's retirement innovation and get inspired. Fear not. My ideas have been tested, time and again, and there should be no ifs, ands, or buts. You're now armed with my ideas and true-life personal experiences in the making. Therefore, it would be prudent to act now (start planning) rather than later.

What Is the Advanced Stage of Retirement?

The advanced stage of retirement (ASOR, pronounced as A-SOR) is a process of providing generous accolade to yourself by enhancing the retirement innovation to owning superior retirement real-estate acquisitions with bigger cash flows. At this stage, you are on your way to being out of your day job; you are fully qualified to move on to the ASOR, a very prestigious place to be in your golden years. I suppose if you retired early you may not prefer to move on to this last stage. It may make sense, depending on the lifestyle you choose. If you were able to attain the gold standard secret before age fifty and have enough cash flow, you may explore a host of other avenues, or really drum up the business to ASOR. Be sure you know what you are in for if you choose to move to ASOR. Make the move in a slow, gradual, and surefire manner. I highly recommend that you move on to ASOR.

There are three owning categories at the ASOR level:

- One five-plus-unit apartment house complex; OR,
- One piece of commercial real estate; OR,

- One piece of property with an absolute NNN Lease.

Starting something small can sometimes lead to a host of other opportunities. Sure enough, ASOR is the place to be. You will be building a commercial real-estate empire by aquiring such acquisitions and developments through the ASOR. The self-made real-estate business is not something static but something that constantly grows (equity advance) through choice of actions (in years) (e.g., forced appreciation). The proper use of this equity advance is the basis of my business model. This is the way to create big in the ASOR. For your small business, you may have to think outside the box and drum up the business to ASOR in a sure-fire way. Creating retirement income without limits. ASOR is at the climax of retirement excellence.

Wisdom of Doing a 1031 Tax-Deferred Exchange

I can buy a larger retirement income property (like kind) by exchanging it with my fourplex, triplex, or duplex. The definition of a 1031 Tax Deferred Exchange is: a method of deferring capital gains tax by exchanging one real property for another like kind property. Other names used for this exchange are: tax deferred exchange, starker exchange, or delayed exchange.

Instead of selling my investment property and owing capital gains tax, I can enter into a tax-deferred exchange for another like kind of investment property.

To defer tax (IRS Rules):

- Replacement property must be identified within forty-five days.
- New property must be acquired within 180 days.

These time limits may force me to rush into a poor investment. This means I will first find my desired property and then I will sell my undesired property. This way I will be able to find the property where tenants pay for all utility expenses, including water and garbage. Or better still, a Triple Net Lease (an absolute NNN Lease or Net Net Net Lease): a type of lease in which the tenant pays all operating expenses (OE) of the property.

An absolute NNN Lease - Tenant Pays All OE:

1. Maintenance (repairs, utilities, janitorial services, license fees)
2. Insurance
3. Property taxes

The owner receives the net rent and pays for debt service (if any). These leases are common for industrial and commercial properties. I plan on purchasing fourplexes, townhouses, or apartment houses, do forced appreciation, and then exchange them with office buildings, drug stores, retail centers, medical buildings, or shopping centers until I have built my desired net worth into a sizable estate.

To Further Your Education It Is Important to Grow

Being motivated through inspirational confidence building, using time-tested device, and actively seeking better nest eggs through education and innovation are the keys to sustaining success in your golden years. Make your further education a stepping-stone, a catalyst, and an essential part of growing your knowledge base. That said, I have developed reading habits to motivate myself, to educate myself and to unlock the door to a world of innovations and opportunities. I promised to myself, "If I take full responsibility for myself, I'll develop a desire to realize my dreams." I have developed an affection for investing in real estate even in my retirement days. Remember, the super rich never really retire. They are "retired at birth." Their retirement is a way of living. I keep educating myself and keep looking for groundbreaking ways with a unique vision to enhance my retirement income stream, as I did for this masterwork book. My plan is to achieve financial independence for myself and my loved ones by creating my own financial dynasty through real-estate retirement investment. With commercial real-estate investment, it only takes one successful deal one time to change your life forever in creating generations and generations of wealth, and also programming the subconscious mind-set of future generations and generations to come.

Conclusion

Our PSORI is certainly our golden eggs and has definite level of retirement excellence. This may be the beginning of the end of being a member of the financially underprivileged middle class, especially in your golden years. Go ahead, inspire yourself by saying, "The best is yet to come in my life," because fortune favors the brave in creating a sustained success through the wisdom of this book.

The true wisdom that I have learned, at ASOR, is that there is more to life than just making money endlessly. Enough is enough. There is a limit. Be in command of money; don't let money be in command of you. Therefore, financial management is the key and know your limit. I learned that money isn't the key to lifetime happiness, although it plays a mighty, mighty role, only if I have developed the esteem and the safeguards to handle it admirably and wisely. In all honesty, brilliant success and bursting happiness go hand in hand. Conversely, I suspect the biggest causal factor to our unhappiness is the lack of money, and we worry about money more as we grow older with insufficient retirement funds. Prior to writing this book, I helped a few coworkers become retirement rich, and now I have dedicated myself to helping many others, including you, my associate.

From the bottom of my heart, I look forward to saying all the best, and the best of health and retirement success!

> *May God bless us in all our endeavors. And may the divine blessings empower us. And again, please don't forget to thank God for creating generations and generations of wealth for you and your loved ones.*

Inspirational Confidence Building

"I am a part of all I have read."

—John Kieran

"Believe one who has tried it."

—Virgil

"If you're going to be thinking, you may as well think big."

—Donald Trump

"Knowledge of what is possible is the beginning of happiness."

—George Santayana

"Work as if everything depended upon work and pray as if everything depended upon prayer."

—William Booth

List of Secrets

The purpose of this list is to help you remember some of the main points in this book.

Author's Final Words

Author's Heart of Gold Prayer:

Our Lord, in your hand is all good. Our Lord, please bestow your blessings so that this book is successfully delivered into the hands of every person you desire, especially the middle class. Our Lord, ease the financial burden and bless the reader who is seeking your pleasure by learning the wisdom of this book. Amen.

Author's Personal Inspirational Mottos:

- Cash is king, but cash flow is retirement king.
- Be in command of money; don't let money be in command of you.
- An absolute NNN Lease property is the ultimate passive stream of retirement income.
- Out of frustration come up with innovation and engage in prosperity thinking.

Author's online Web site:

www.RetireLucky.com

Abbreviations

(a) — Annual

AC — Acquisition Cost

ASOR — Advanced Stage of Retirement

AOA — Apartment Owners Association

APR — Annual Percentage Rate

ARM — Adjustable Rate Mortgage

CD — Certificate of Deposit

CF — Cash Flow

COCR — Cash-on-Cash Return

COE — Close of Escrow

CR — Capitalization Rate

DCR — Debt Coverage Ratio

DS — Debt Service

ERI — Expandable Retirement Income (Realtors call it Expandable Rental Income or Expandable Income)

FDA — U. S. Food and Drug Administration

FDR — Franklin D. Roosevelt

FICO — Fair Isaac Corporation

GRM — Gross Rent Multiplier

G&E— Gas and Electricity

Inc. — Incorporated

LLC —Limited Liability Company

LTV — Loan-to-Value Ratio

MLS — Multiple Listing Service

NORI — Net Operating Retirement Income (Realtors call it Net Operating Rental Income or Net Operating Income)

NNN Lease — Triple Net Lease

OE — Operating Expenses

OPM — Other People's Money

P. O. — Post Office

PSORI — Passive Stream of Retirement Income (Realtors call it Passive Stream of Rental Income or Passive Stream of Income or Gross Schedule Rental Income or Gross Rental Income or Gross Income)

PTC — Prospective Tenant Card

QA — Quality Assurance

SASE — Self-Addressed Stamped Envelope

SFR — Single Family Residence

SP — Selling Price

SRI — Spendable Retirement Income (Realtors call it Spendable Rental Income or Spendable Income)

TSP — Thrift Savings Plan

YTD — Year to Date

Glossary

A

Adjustable Rate Mortgage (ARM) — A mortgage loan that allows the interest rate to be changed at specific intervals that are tied to some index plus margin over the life of the loan. ARMs start at teaser rates (lower than market rate), then adjust at specific intervals as spelled out in the promissory note. Caution: There is a risk associated with ARM loans since most are geared to rise above the fixed interest after the teaser term expires.

Agency — The legal representation of a seller or a buyer. Some states, such as California, require agency disclosure when making a purchase offer. Be aware that if you are making a purchase offer through a listing agent, he/she may have to represent both parties in the transaction, a so-called dual agency. The question is: is the listing agent doing his/her fiduciary duty to the buyer or the seller? Caution: In most cases, the agent represents the principal, the seller!

Agent — A licensed real-estate broker or a licensed sales associate or sales agent (also see broker and sales associate).

Amortization — A term used in mortgage payment calculation. When the loan is fully amortized, the gradual monthly mortgage payment, including interest, should decrease a portion of the principal balance monthly. A thirty-year fully amortized loan, after 360 mortgage payments are made, should have a principal balance (loan) of zero. Normally, a loan is amortized for fifteen years, thirty years, or forty years. Of course, a forty-year loan will have a lower monthly mortgage payment.

Anchor Tenant — A main tenant in a shopping center.

Annual Percentage Rate (APR) — The Truth in Lending Act (Regulation Z) requires lenders to truthfully quote APR in ads so that borrowers are aware of the effective interest rate (in percent) of the amount financed. This includes loan origination fee, discount points, and broker commission (if any). When shopping for a loan, please compare the interest rate with the APR from different lenders.

Appraisal — An opinion of the current market value (estimate of value) of a property. The formal estimate of value of the property is done by a certified appraiser. (Also see Appraiser)

Appraiser — A certified appraiser is a person who renders an opinion of current market value of a property in a formal writing (short form or long form). An appraiser may be called upon for expert testimony in regards to his/her appraisal work in a court of law.

Appreciation — An increase in the value of the property due to any cause. (Also see Forced Appreciation.)

"As is" — A term used when making an offer to purchase a property. The property is sold "as is," meaning the property is sold in its present condition and the seller is off the hook for doing any repairs or improvements.

Asking Price — It is the same as listing price, the price the seller wants. The price offered (offered price) can be the selling price or listing price if the seller accepts the price offered (accepted price). Please note: seller's asking price may not be fair market price.

Asset — Anything that has value: houses, cars, land, securities, bank deposits, cash, stocks and bonds, promissory notes, and mortgages.

B

Balloon Payment — A lump-sum payment of a mortgaged loan. A loan that is amortized for thirty to forty years but that is due in three to ten years ends up with a balloon payment to pay off the loan.

Beneficiary — A person or family group (heirs) who will benefit from the passive stream of retirement income (PSORI) or from sale of the property as set by the trustor in a trust or a will.

Broker — A licensed real-estate agent who employs sales associates or sales agents. A broker charges a commission (fee) for negotiating a real estate sale and is normally paid by the seller.

Buyer's Agent — A licensed real-estate agent who works for a broker as a sales associates or sales agent. The buyer's agent does not charge for his/her service. If the property is sold, the buyer's agent gets paid by the broker who receives the commission from the seller. Normally, the buyer's agent receives one-quarter of the commission split.

Buyer's Broker — A licensed real-estate agent who represents the buyer in a transaction. The buyer's broker does not charge for his/her service. If the property is sold, the buyer's broker gets paid by the listing broker, who receives the commission from the seller.

C

Capital Expenses (Capital Expenditure) — An improvement (not repair work done) that has a useful life of more than one year. Examples include: new carpet, new blinds, new appliances, new roof, new asphalt on the driveway, any new fixtures, and so on and so forth. The IRS allows capital expenses to be deducted (depreciated) over its useful life rather than counted as a regular expense in the current year.

Capital Gains — The profit made on the sale of an investment, which may be taxable.

Capitalization Rate (cap rate or CR) — It is the rate-of-return on a retirement investment. In other words, it is a way of valuing our purchase offer of a property by use of the net operating retirement income (NORI), to the probability of finding the risk factor associated with a retirement investment. A cap rate is a property's expected annual NORI(a) expressed as a percentage of a buyer's retirement investment (i.e., the cap rate is calculated by dividing NORI(a) by the purchase price (value of property) and multiplying it by 100). Cap rate only accounts for return from NORI and not from property appreciation. Note: this is good since this book does not consider property appreciation a means of PSORI.

$$CR = \frac{NORI_{(a)}}{V} \times 100$$

CR = Cap Rate (%); NORI = Net Operating Retirement Income; V = Value (of Property); $_{(a)}$ = Annual

Cash flow — Cash flow (synonymous with the words: positive cash flow) is simply defined as the money left over for the super rich after paying all the operating expenses (OE) of the business transactions in a month, which is theirs to keep or spend as they wish. Cash flow is the main power house for the super rich. Cash flow is also called expandable retirement income or spendable retirement income. The source of expandable retirement income initially comes from passive stream of retirement income (PSORI) also called gross schedule retirement rental income. After paying operating expenses ($OE_{(a)}$), the super rich get net operating retirement income ($NORI_{(a)}$), and then after paying the debt service ($DS_{(a)}$), the super rich get cash flow (CF). CF is normally reported as an annual figure (multiply by 12).

$$CF = NORI_{(a)} - DS_{(a)}$$

CF = cash flow; NORI = net operating retirement income; DS = debt service; $_{(a)}$ = annual

Cash-on-Cash Return (COCR) — A calculation that gives a percent profit return on investment to the cash contributed toward the investment. First, calculate the cash flow (CF) and then divide by the acquisition cost (AC) and multiply by 100 to get percent cash-on-cash return.

COCR:

$$CF = NORI_{(a)} - DS_{(a)}$$

$$COCR = \frac{CF}{AC} \times 100$$

COCR = cash-on-cash return; CF = cash flow; NORI = net operating retirement income; DS = debt service; $_{(a)}$ = annual; AC = acquisition cost

Caveat Emptor — A Latin legal term used when purchasing, meaning "Let the buyer beware."

Clear Title — A title without liens on the property.

Commercial Loan — A mortgage loan for five or more units, or multi-family apartment house complexes, including a mortgage on commercial or industrial property.

Commercial Property — Any business use property or five or more units of multi-family apartment house complexes including office, retail, industrial, warehouse, and land. (Also see strip mall.)

Commission — A broker's fee for service.

Conventional Loan — A real estate mortgage loan that is neither Federal Housing Administration insured, nor Veteran's Assistance guaranteed.

D

Debt Coverage Ratio (DCR) — This is a ratio of annual net operating retirement income ($NORI_{(a)}$) to annual debt service ($DS_{(a)}$). It measures the $NORI_{(a)}$ relative to $DS_{(a)}$. The DCR ratio is powerful ratio figure that shows strength of cash flow. DCR of 1.00 clearly shows the breakeven point, where there is neither positive cash flow or negative cash flow. DCR of 2.00 shows strong cash flow, whereas 0.50 shows a negative cash flow.

DCR Ratio Formula:

$$DCR = \frac{NORI_{(a)}}{DS_{(a)}}$$

DCR 0.50 = Negative CF

DCR 1.00 = *Break Even*

DCR 2.00 = Strong CF

DCR = Debt Coverage Ratio; NORI = Net Operating Retirement Income; $_{(a)}$ = Annual; DS = Debt Service; CF = Cash Flow

Debt Service — Total mortgage payments, annually or monthly as required.

Deed — A formal written document, which is used to transfer ownership of title of a property from the seller to the buyer or from one owner to another. It is also referred to as grant deed, since it is granted from the grantor (seller) to the grantee (buyer).

Deed of Trust (Trust Deed) — A formal written document signed by the borrower (buyer), which is secured by a promissory note on the property, which authorizes a trustee (third party) to hold the title to a property until all the payments satisfy the loan. Once the borrower completes payment of the debt (loan) in full, the title of the property is transferred to the buyer via an instrument called deed of reconveyance. Note: having purchased a fourplex and holding a deed of reconveyance in hand is truly the gold standard secret!

Delayed Exchange — See Tax Deferred Exchange.

Down Payment — A certain amount of cash payment that a buyer (borrower) must pay before a lender will give a mortgage for the balance. The lender requires a certain percent of the seller's accepted price.

Due Diligence — A clause in the purchase contract that permits the buyer a specified period of time to research a property, including inspections, before a final decision is made to purchase the property. Use due diligence to find the strengths and defects in the property before making an informed decision.

Due-on-Sale Clause — The clause states, the balance of the mortgage principal is due-on-sale of the property (i.e., in the event of a sale of the property, a provision in a mortgage contract that states the full outstanding loan balance is due to the lender). The outstanding loan amount must be paid to the lender at the close of escrow.

Duplex — Two dwelling units sharing one common roof, or two dwelling units situated on one lot.

E

Earnest Money — When making an offer to purchase a property, a buyer includes a small amount of money in the form of a check as a deposit to show good faith to the seller. If the offer is accepted, the check is deposited in an escrow account and applied toward the purchase price.

Equity — It is a portion of value of the property that belongs to the owner. It is the difference between the market value of the property and the total amount of debt against it. Equity can change upon the market condition. It is dependent on supply and demand. If I have no debt against the property, I essentially have 100 percent equity. It is also known as sweet equity.

Escheat — is defined as the reversion of property back to the state government in the event that the property owner dies without a written will or trust and has no legal heirs.

Escrow — A neutral third party that holds custody of all contractual instruments for safekeeping until certain conditions are met. The third party is usually a title company or a lawyer. The earnest money deposit, deeds, title report, so on and so forth are said to be "placed in escrow account" at the escrow. The escrow serves as a clearing house for all matters pertaining to the sale and purchase of the property until all items are satisfied before closing.

Escrow Agent — An escrow officer or a lawyer who is a neutral third party handling escrow work.

Eviction — Eviction (tenant eviction) means removing the tenant (lessee) from the premises by way of legal processing and recovering possession of the property.

Expandable Retirement Income — see cash flow.

F

Fee Simple Estate — An absolute ownership of a property.

FICO Scores — A FICO Score is a credit score, a number that lenders use to measure credit risk or creditworthiness of a borrower by looking at the borrower's credit report.

Categorizing FICO Scores:

- Over 720—Excellent
- 680-720—Very Good
- 620-680—Borderline
- 620-below—Not Good

Fiduciary Responsibility — A requirement for full disclosure of material facts.

Fixed Expenses — Taxes and insurance are fixed recurring expenses.

Fixed Rate Loan — A mortgage loan payment that does not change over the life of the loan. The rate of interest is fixed.

Forced Appreciation — An increase in the value of the property due to making certain improvements. By doing forced appreciation to a property, the owner will gain sweat equity. (Also see appreciation and sweat equity.)

Fourplex — Four dwelling units sharing one common roof or four dwelling units situated on one lot.

Free-and-clear-title — There are no liens against a property, neither a mortgage nor a tax lien.

Fully Amortized — See Amortization.

G

Gross Rent Multiplier (GRM) — A ratio giver. It is way to compare properties for sale. A calculation that gives me passive stream of retirement income (PSORI) to selling price ratio, (i.e. GRM measures the annual $PSORI_{(a)}$ relative to the selling price. Caution: GRM does not in any way indicate the condition of the property. If a calculation equals a GRM of twelve, it indicates sale price is twelve times the annual $PSORI_{(a)}$.

$$GRM = \frac{SP}{PSORI_{(a)}}$$

GRM = gross rent multiplier; SP = selling price;
PSORI = passive stream of retirement income;
$_{(a)}$ = annual

Gross Schedule Retirement Rental Income — See Passive Stream of Retirement Income (PSORI).

H

Highest and Best Use — An appraisal term used to indicate its greatest net return to the land and/or the building over a given period. In its highest and best use, zoning laws play a significant role, especially for vacant undeveloped land.

HVAC — Heating, Ventilation, Air Conditioning.

I

Investment — Ownership of real estate for passive stream of retirement income (PSORI).

Irrevocable Living Trust —A trust that may not be revised or terminated by the trustor once the agreement is signed.

J

Joint Tenancy — A title ownership issued to two or more persons. A title held as joint tenants has the right of survivorship with an undivided interest. Ownership of a property in joint tenancy means that each tenant can inherit the property fully if the other one dies.

L

Landlord — The owner of a property who rents property to another. The landlord is a lessor. The tenant is a lessee. A landlord is a property owner (lessor) who surrenders the right to use property (to a lessee) for a specific time in exchange for the receipt of rent.

Lease — A formal written contract between landlord and tenant may be called a rental agreement and/or lease. It enables the premises to be used as a dwelling by tenant in return for rent.

Lessee — The tenant is a lessee.

Lessor — The landlord is a lessor.

Leverage — The use of borrowed money to purchase an investment; (1) to increase purchasing power, and (2) to ultimately increase the profitability of an investment (increase one's yield). The term is synonymous with the use of other people's money (OPM).

Lien — A lien is a type of encumbrance. It is a claim against the property as security for the payment of a debt. All liens are satisfied upon sale of a property. A lien can be voluntary or involuntary. A mortgage is a voluntary lien. Some involuntary liens are tax lien, mechanic lien, judgment lien, and general lien.

Limited Liability Company (LLC) — This is a legal business entity registered with the Secretary of State. It is the simplest and the best form of legal business structure for a small real-estate business. LLC is not used to protect a business entity but rather to protect personal assets from malicious litigation. LLC takes the property owner's name off the radar screen, so to speak.

Listing — A signed contract authorizing a broker to sell or lease a property.

Listing Broker — A broker who has a signed contract with a seller to list and sell the property. Also a broker who has a signed contract with a landlord to list and rent the property on behalf of the landlord.

Living Will/Advance Health Care Directives —A written document that clearly states to caregivers, in advance, a person's decision whether or not they want to be kept on an artificial life support.

Loan-to-Value Ratio (LTV) — A term used by lenders. It is the ratio of a portion of the amount borrowed compared to the purchase price. A 70 percent LTV means a lender requires 30 percent down payment.

M

Mortgage — A recorded written loan contract that makes a specific property a security for payment of a specified debt. It is a lien on the property.

Note: essentially, a mortgage is a loan backed by real property. As a borrower, you give a mortgage on your property to the lender, which pledges your property as collateral, and the lender gives you a loan in return.

Multiple Listing Service (MLS) — This is an association of real-estate brokers and sales associates who agree to share listings with one another. The commission is also shared among the listing and selling broker.

N

NNN Lease — (Net Net Net Lease) See Triple Net Lease.

Net Operating Retirement Income (NORI) — (Realtors call it net operating rental income or net operating income). It is a retirement income before paying mortgage payments. I locate my NORI by first finding my total passive stream of retirement income (PSORI) for the month, also called Gross Schedule Retirement Rental Income. After paying Operating Expenses (OE) it incurred for the month, I get my NORI. I multiply by twelve to get my annual figure for the formula. For some super rich, NORI = expandable retirement income instead of cash flow (CF).

$$NORI_{(a)} = PSORI_{(a)} - OE_{(a)}$$

NORI = Net Operating Retirement Income;
PSORI = Passive Stream of Retirement Income;
OE = Operating Expenses;
$_{(a)}$ = Annual

O

Operating Expenses (OE) — All expenses associated to run the rental property, except the debt service (mortgage payments).

OPM —Other people's money. The term is synonymous with the word leverage. The use of borrowed money to purchase an investment; (1) to increase purchasing power, and (2) ultimately increase the profitability of an investment.

P

Passive Stream of Retirement Income (PSORI) — (Realtors call it passive stream of rental income or passive stream of income or gross schedule rental income or gross schedule income or gross income). It is total amount of rental revenue collected in a month from a rented property. It is normally reported as an annual figure ($PSORI_{(a)}$). It is also called gross schedule retirement rental income.

Preliminary Title Report — A title search report issued by the title company or by a lawyer determining the legal ownership, chain of title, mortgage lien, easements, covenants, and conditions of the property. In California, a preliminary title report search is a must before title insurance is issued by a title company.

Pro Forma — A financial statement showing what is expected to occur with cash flow in future years. It is written by a real-estate broker or sales associate for a prospective buyer and gives financial projections. Caution: in pro forma cash flow statements, figures are grossly exaggerated to show positive cash flow. Be careful to use realistic figures, especially for passive stream of retirement income (PSORI).

Promissory Note (Note) — A formal written document (agreement) signed by a borrower (buyer) who acknowledges a debt and promises (hence, promissory note) to pay a specified sum of money with certain conditions at a specified time. For lender's protection, the note is secured by the deed of trust.

Q

QA — Quality Assurance

Quiet Enjoyment (Quiet Title Enjoyment) — A right of a property owner or any other legally entitled individual to the use of the property without undue interference.

R

Ready, Willing, and Able Buyer — A buyer who is prepared, who knows the nuts and bolts of real estate (ready) on agreed terms (willing) and has the financial qualifications to do so (able).

Realtor — A licensed real-estate broker who belongs to the National Association of Realtors.

Recording — An act of entering in a book of public records at the county recorder's office affecting the title of the property, giving a factual notice to the general public.

Rental Agreement and/or Lease — See Lease.

Revocable Living Trust — A trust that may be revised or revoked at any time by the trustor or trustors who created it.

S

Sales Associate — A licensed salesperson or sales agent who works for a real-estate broker.

Setback — A word used by city zoning ordinance to mean the distance from the property line to an established line within which no building or attached structure may be erected.

Starker Exchange — see Tax Deferred Exchange.

Spendable Retirement Income — see cash flow (Realtors call it spendable rental income or spendable income).

Strip Mall (Commercial Strip) — This is a retail building having small and big commercial tenants but no anchor tenant.

Sweat Equity — This is also called forced equity. This term is synonymous with the word equity, except that the value added to a property is due to improvements as a result of work performed by the owner or by a hired contractor. Equity: it is that portion of value of the property that belongs to the owner. It is the difference between market value of the property and the total amount of debt against it. Equity can change upon market conditions. It is dependent on supply and demand. If you have no debt against a property, you essentially have 100 percent equity!

Sweet Equity — See Equity.

T

Tax Deferred Exchange — Other names used such as: 1031 Tax Deferred Exchange or starker exchange or delayed exchange. It is a method of deferring capital gains tax by exchanging it with a real property for another like kind of property.

Tax Depreciation Deduction — A form of tax deduction for depreciable real estate. It is subject to an allowance for depreciation under the Internal Revenue Code. A straight-line method is used for a twenty-seven-and-a-half-year remaining depreciable life.

Tenancy-in-Common — A title ownership issue for two or more persons. A title held as tenants-in-common can have divided and undivided interests. If one person dies, that person's interest goes to heirs of the deceased and not to the other tenant-in-common.

Tenant — A person who occupies premises and pays rent under a written lease agreement or even under verbal agreement.

Title Insurance — An insurance policy to protect the buyer and the lender for any loss sustained by defect in the title. This a one-time insurance premium (nonrecurring cost) paid by the buyer at close of escrow. The title company insures it until the property is re-sold.

Title Report — See Preliminary Title Report.

Townhouse — A house that shares at least one wall with another house. Or single family residences (SFR) attached to other similar SFRs via party walls.

Transfer Disclosure Statement — The seller completes this form to disclose any knowledge he/she has about the property. Some states do not require this, but I know the State of California does. It is given to the buyer immediately after the offer ratification.

Triple Net Lease (An absolute NNN Lease or Net Net Net Lease) — A type of lease in which the tenant pays all operating expenses (OE) for the property, including:

- Maintenance (repairs, utilities, janitorial services, license fees)
- Insurance
- Property taxes

The owner receives the net rent and pays for debt service (if any). These leases are common for industrial, office, and retail commercial properties.

Triplex — Three dwelling units sharing one common roof or three dwelling units in one lot.

Trust — A written legal document (an agreement) whereby property or money is transferred to another party upon certain conditions set forth by the givers (trustors). Trust is an enforceable document of how a person wishes his or her property to be distributed without a probate court, whereas a will still requires a probate court ruling. To make this a legal trust, it should involve three parties, namely, a trustor, trustee, and beneficiary.

Trustor —A person who provides a property and creates a trust.

Trustee —A nominated person (even the trustor) or bank or organization that holds the title of the trust property and offers specially trained administrators to provide counseling and tax services. Important note: most people name themselves as the trustee in charge of managing their trust assets until they become incompetent or die. My wife and I are both trustors and trustees (grantors) for the revocable living trust.

Trust Deed (Deed of Trust) — See Deed of Trust.

W

Will — This is simply a written document stating how you want your assets to be divided when you die. A holographic will is a completely handwritten will.

1031 Tax Deferred Exchange — See Tax Deferred Exchange

Appendix A

Appendix A-1

Unit Rent Receivable Log

_______________ (Property Address) _______________

_______________ (Name of Tenants) _______________

	(Year)	CHECK #	DATE RECEIVED	RENT AMOUNT	TOTAL YTD
1	January				
2	February				
3	March				
4	April				
5	May				
6	June				
7	July				
8	August				
9	September				
10	October				
11	November				
12	December				

Property rented date:	
Security deposit received ($):	
Last rent increased date: Amount increased ($_______________)	
Proposed rent increase date: (Notification Date**:**_______________)	
% Rent increase:	

Notes____

Appendix A-2

Unit Rental History Log

_____________(Property Address with unit #)_____________________

____

DATE	RENT AMOUNT	DATE	RENT AMOUNT

Appendix A-3

Operating Expenses Log
(For a Single Property)

__________(Your Property Address)__________________

____

Date	Name of Store/Contractor	TOTAL	TOTAL YTD

Appendix A-4

City and County Expenses Log
(For a Single Property)

(Your Property Address)

City and County Expenses
(County Health Inspections, Fire Department, etc.)

Date	Name of Department & Purpose of Inspection	TOTAL	TOTAL YTD

Appendix A-5

Capital Expenses Log
(For a Single Property)

__________(Your Property Address)____________________
____
____

Capital Expenses
(new carpet, new blinds, new appliances, new roof, new asphalt on the driveway, any new fixtures, etc.)

Date	Name of Store/Contractor	TOTAL	TOTAL YTD

Appendix A-6

Schedule E Log
(For recording totals for Schedule E (Tax Return) for the year)

Operating Expenses

TRANSACTION	TOTAL
Advertising	
Cleaning and Maintenance	
Commissions	
Repairs	
Legal and other Professional Fees	
Supplies	
Insurance	
Property Tax	
Utilities—(Water, Garbage, G&E)	
Miles	
City/County Inspections	
Bank Charges	
License	
Postage	
Telephone	

OTHERS (LIST):	
Mortgage Interest Paid	
Capital Expenses—(New carpet, new blinds, new appliances, new roof, new asphalt on the driveway, etc.)	

Appendix B

(The Superpower Tools)

Appendix B-1

Addendum to Notice of Changes in Terms of Tenancy

To___(Name of tenants)_______ tenant and others in possession of the premises situated at __(full address)____

Notice is hereby given that the terms of the rental agreement by which you hold possession of the above premises will be changed as follows:

Changes:

- Effective____(date)____, the above premises have been purchased by:

  ____(Your Name)_____

- Please make rental check payable to:

  (Your name)
  Payment Processing
  (Your full address)

- No cash payment will be accepted.

Twelve self-addressed stamped envelopes are provided herewith for your convenience.

Other changes: none.

Discount program:

If a tenant's rent payment envelope is postmarked on or before__28th__of each month for the whole year (at least 10 rent payments), that tenant will receive a reward check of ___$(amount)___, one month before Christmas from (Your Name). Additionally, if a tenant's rent payment envelope is postmarked on or before ___30th___of each month for the whole year (at least 10 rent payments), that tenant will receive a reward check of ___$(amount)___, one month before Christmas from (Your name).

Drain stoppages:

Water flow blockages are tenant's responsibility when caused by their own carelessness and/or negligence. Tenants will pay for any drain stoppages when caused by unnatural causes. This includes clogged toilets, clogged showers, clogged bathroom sinks or kitchen sinks, and clogged washing machine outlets.

If the work is performed by the landlord's plumber or by a hired plumber, the property manager will provide tenants with a ___copy of the bill___ showing the work performed by the plumber in addition to ___$ (amount)___ management fees via U. S. mail.

Payment of rent:

(Your name) has a strict policy of collecting late fees and evicting if rent is not paid on time. Late fees accrue if your rent payment is not received by the___5th___day of the month (post marked by 5th of the month). In addition, if your rent payment is not received by the___5th___day of the month (post marked by 5th of the month). (Your name)'s collection attorney will seek collection and eviction and will report the unpaid rent to credit reporting agencies. (Your name) hopes this never happens, so please pay your rent on time.

Time is of the essence and no excuses (ill health, job loss, financial emergency, etc.) will be accepted for late rent payment.

Rent payment late charge—after 5th day:

A late fee of___$ (amount)___, said amount not to exceed 6%

of the monthly rent, shall be an additional payment if not received by the____5th___day of the month (payment envelope post marked by 5th of the month). Attach a separate check of___$ (amount)__ payable to _(your name)___

Any rent lost in the postal mail will be treated as unpaid until received by (your name).

Rent payment late charge—beginning on 10th day:

Rental payment received on or after the___10th__ of the month will incur additional per day penalty. A late fee of _$15.00 per day penalty_ will apply in addition to initial late fee of__$ (amount)_ (above). Attach a separate check of___$ (amount)__ plus___$15.00 per day penalty__ payable to _(your name)____

Any rent lost in the mail will be treated as unpaid until received by (your name).

Garbage throwing/recycling rules:

(Name of city) in coordination (Garbage hauling Co.—if any) with County Environmental Health Services requires strict adherence to the rules below: Rule # 1: Kitchen garbage must be placed inside the city garbage container. Do not leave anything around the container. Rule # 2: Recyclable kitchen products must be placed in its marked container. Rule # 3: All cardboard boxes must be cut in suitable sizes to be placed in its marked container. Rule # 4: Absolutely no dumping allowed. Furniture or any large item must be taken to disposal site by the tenants themselves. Absolutely no warnings will be issued by the property manager for any violations to the above rule(s). Tenants will be billed___$ (amount)__ fine for any violation of the above rule and/or the cost of hauling the item and addition to ____$25.00_____ administrative fee via U.S. postal mail.

Any violations to the garbage throwing/recycling policy, the tenants will be billed____$100.00_____ fine (in addition to city fine) with ____$25.00_____ administrative fee via U.S. postal mail.

Failure to comply with any of these rules/policies may result in fines and/or tenant's eviction.

Rules and regulations:

Tenants have read and agreed to abide by all rules and regulations of (Your Name) as they presently exist or they may be amended at (Your name)'s sole discretion. Other said Rules and Regulations are attached hereto and are herein incorporated by reference.

Other rules—effective immediately:

Parking areas:

No car washing,

No auto repairs or oil changing,

No junk storage,

No storage of flammable or dangerous materials, and

Tenants will keep all assigned areas clean and neat and free of trash and debris, including parking.

Rent check bounce policy:

If a tenant's rent check bounces 2nd (second) time, (your name) will ask the tenant to send cashier's check or money order at all times. Only after 6 months of non-bounce rent checks can the tenant request in writing for removal of above check policy.

A charge of ____$45.00_____ or the higher amount charged by the bank shall be paid by the tenant for any check that is returned unpaid. Upon return or dishonor of any check tendered as payment of rent, late charges will be assessed as if no rent payment was attempted; therefore, rent payment late charge will apply.

Apartment door—lock and key policy:

Due to emergency need, absolutely no re-keying will be allowed by tenants without prior approval of the property manager. However, tenants can make more keys for their family members as necessary. Due to emergency need, the property manager will re-key to its original key without formal tenant notification. Tenants will be billed __$ (amount)__ fine for any violation of the above policy and addition to ____$25.00____ administrative fee via U.S. postal mail.

Failure to comply with any of these rules/policies may result in fines and/or tenant's eviction.

All other terms of the said rental agreement will remain in full force and effect.

Dated this:______________________________

Signed:________________________________

(Your name)
Property Manager
(Your full street address)
Cell: XXX-XXX-XXXX
Fax: XXX-XXX-XXXX

Appendix B-2

(Addendum to the Rental Agreement and/or Lease)

Addendum to the rental agreement:

This addendum becomes part of the said rental agreement and/or lease between owner and tenants.

Discount program:

If a tenant's rent payment envelope is postmarked on or

before__28th_of each month for the whole year (at least 10 rent payments), that tenant will receive a reward check of__$ (amount) __, one month before Christmas from (your name). Additionally, if a tenant's rent payment envelope is postmarked on or before ___30th__of each month for the whole year (at least 10 rent payments), that tenant will receive a reward check of__$ (amount)__, one month before Christmas from (your name).

Drain stoppages:

Water flow blockages are tenants responsibility when caused by their own carelessness and/or negligence. Tenants will pay for any drain stoppages when caused by unnatural causes. This includes clogged toilets, clogged showers, clogged bathroom sinks and clogged kitchen sinks, and clogged washing machine outlets.

If the work is performed by the landlord's plumber or by a hired plumber, the property manager will provide tenants with a _copy of the bill_ showing the work performed by the plumber in addition to _$ (amount)_ management fees via U. S. mail.

Payment of rent:

(Your name) has a strict policy of collecting late fees and evicting if rent is not paid on time. Late fees accrue if your rent payment is not received by the____5th___day of the month (post marked by 5th of the month). In addition, if your rent payment is not received by the____5th___day of the month (postmarked by 5th of the month). (Your name)'s collection attorney will seek collection and eviction and will report the unpaid rent to credit reporting agencies. (Your name) hopes this never happens, so please pay your rent on time.

Time is of the essence, and no excuses (ill health, job loss, financial emergency, etc.) will be accepted for late rent payment.

Rent payment late charge—after 5th day:

A late fee of___$ (amount)___, said amount not to exceed 6% of the monthly rent, shall be an additional payment if not received by the___5th___day of the month (payment envelope post marked by 5th of the month). Attach a separate check of___$ (amount)___ payable to ___(your name)___

Any rent lost in the postal mail will be treated as unpaid until received by (your name).

Rent payment late charge—beginning on 10th day:

Rental payment received on or after the___10th___ of the month will incur additional per day penalty. A late fee of ___$15.00 per day penalty___ will apply in addition to initial late fee of___$ (amount)___ (above). Attach a separate check of___$ (amount)___ plus___$15.00 per day penalty___ payable to ___(your name)___ Any rent lost in the mail will be treated as unpaid until received by (your name).

Garbage throwing/recycling rules:

(Name of city) in coordination (Garbage hauling Co.—if any) with County Environmental Health Services requires strict adherence to the rules below: Rule # 1: Kitchen garbage must be placed inside the city garbage container. Do not leave anything around the container. Rule # 2: Recyclable kitchen products must be placed in its marked container. Rule # 3: All cardboard boxes must be cut in suitable sizes to be placed in its marked container. Rule # 4: Absolutely no dumping allowed. Furniture or any large item must be taken to disposal site by the tenants themselves. Absolutely no warnings will be issued by the property manager for any violations to the above rule(s). Tenants will be billed___$ (amount)___ fine for any violation of the above rule and/or the cost of hauling the item and addition to ___$25.00___ administrative fee via U.S. postal mail.

Any violations to the garbage throwing/recycling policy, the tenants will be billed___$100.00___ FINE (in addition to

City FINE) with ____$25.00_____ administrative fee via U.S. postal mail.

Failure to comply with any of these rules/policies may result in fines and/or tenant's eviction.

Rules and regulations:

Tenants have read and agreed to abide by all rules and regulations of (your Name) as they presently exist or they may be amended at (your name)'s sole discretion. Other said rules and regulations are attached hereto and are herein incorporated by reference.

Other rules—effective immediately:

Parking areas:

No car washing,

No auto repairs or oil changing,

No junk storage,

No storage of flammable or dangerous materials, and

Tenants will keep all assigned areas clean and neat, and free of trash and debris including parking.

Rent check bounce policy:

If a tenant's rent check bounces 2nd (second) time, (your name) will ask the tenant to send cashier's check or money order at all times. Only after 6 months of non-bounce rent checks that a tenant can request in writing for removal of above check policy.

A charge of ____$45.00_____ or the higher amount charged by the bank shall be paid by the tenant for any check that is returned unpaid. Upon return or dishonor of any check tendered as payment of rent, late charges will be assessed as if no rental payment was attempted; therefore, rent payment late charge will apply.

Apartment door—lock and key policy:

Due to emergency need, absolutely no re-keying will be allowed by tenants without prior approval of the property manager. However, tenants can make more keys for their family members as necessary. Due to emergency need, the property manager will re-key to its original key without formal tenant notification. Tenants will be billed

__$ (amount)__fine for any violation of the above policy and addition to ____$25.00____ administrative fee via U.S. postal mail.

All other terms of the said Rental Agreement will remain in full force and effect.

Dated this: ____________________________

____

(Print—tenant name)

____

(Signature)

____

(Print—tenant name)

____

(Signature)

____

(Your Name)
Property Manager
Cell phone: XXX-XXX-XXXX (Emergency only)

Appendix B-3

Rent Increase Letter (Format)
(Your Address)

Date: (Date)
To: (Tenant Name(s) & Address of the Property)
From: (Your Name & (Title)—Property Manager)
Subject: Addendum to Notice of
Change in Terms of Tenancy
Account #: (Unit #/Year)

certified mail # xxxx xxxx xxxx

Notice is hereby given that 60 (sixty) days after service upon above parties or (date) whichever is later, the terms of said rental agreement by which tenants and others holding possession of the above premises will be changed as follows:

1. The rent will be $ (amount) per month, payable in advance upon the 1st day of each calendar month, instead of $ (amount)

2. other changes: none.

All other terms of the rental agreement will remain in full force and effect.

Dated this (date) ________________

By ____________________
(Your Name)
Property Manager

Appendix B-4

Rent Unpaid Beyond Grace Period (Format)
(Your Address)

Date: (Date)
To: (Tenant Name(s) & Address of the Property)
From: (Your Name & (Title)—Property Manager)
Subject: (Month, Year)—Rent
Unpaid Beyond Grace Period
Account #: (Unit #/Year)

You are in violation of terms of the said Rental Agreement, which states, in part,

"Terms: resident agrees to pay in advance $ (amount) per month on the ___1 st___ day of each month."

You are also in violation of the rent payment late charge of the said rental agreement, which states, in part, "A late fee of ___$ (amount)___, said amount not to exceed 6% of the monthly rent, shall be an additional payment if not received by the___5th___day of the month (post marked by 5th of the month).

Particulars of transactions

Rent amount for the month of (Month), (Year).........$ (amount)
Rent payment late charge...$ (amount)
Total rent amount that was due for (Month), (Year)...$ (amount)

Please Note: The above amount is due upon receipt.

If the above amount is not postmarked (self-addressed stamped envelope) on or before 2nd day of delivery of this notice, (your name)'s collection attorney will seek collection and may lead to eviction. Time is of the essence, and no excuses (ill health, job loss, financial emergency, etc.) will be accepted for late rent payment.

(Your name), Property Manager, Cell: XXX-XXX-XXXX (Emergency Only)

Return this portion with your payment. Thank you.
Please make check payable to: (your name)

TRANSACTION		TOTAL AMOUNT DUE
Tenant: (Name), (Complete address) Rent amount for the month of (Month), (Year).........$ (amount) Rent payment late charge..$ (amount) Total rent amount that was due for (Month), (Year)..**$ (amount)**		**$ (amount)**
Account #:(Unit #/Year)	**Billing Date: (Date)**	**Due Date: Due upon receipt**

Appendix B-5

Partial Rent Payment Letter (Format)
(Your Address)

Date: (Date)
To: (Tenant Name(s) & Address of the Property)
From: (Your Name & (Title)—Property Manager)
Subject: (Month, Year)—Partial Payment
Account #: (Unit #/Year)

You are in violation of terms of the said rental agreement, which states, in part,

"terms: resident agrees to pay in advance $ (amount) per month on the 1 st day of each month."

Particulars of transactions

Rent amount for the month of (Month), (Year).......$ (amount)
Less rent amount received, (date), (Check #)........$ (amount)

Amount of (Month), (Year) rent due.................. $ (amount)

Please Note: The above amount is due upon receipt.

If the above amount is not postmarked (self-addressed stamped envelope) on or before 2nd day of delivery of this notice, <u>(your name)</u>'s collection attorney will seek collection and may lead to eviction. Time is of the essence, and no excuses (ill health, job loss, financial emergency, etc.) will be accepted for late rent payment.

<u>(Your name)</u>, Property Manager, Cell: XXX-XXX-XXXX (Emergency Only)

- -

Return this portion with your payment. Thank you.
Please make check payable to: (Your Name)

TRANSACTION	**TOTAL AMOUNT DUE**
Tenant: (Name), (Complete address) Rent amount for the month of (Month), (Year).......$ (amount) **<u>LESS</u>** rent amount received, (date), (Check #)........<u>$ (amount)</u> Amount of (Month), (Year) rent due..................**$ (amount)**	**$ (amount)**
Account #:(Unit #/Year) **Billing Date: (Date)**	**Due Date: Due upon receipt**

Appendix B-6

Drain Stoppages Fee Letter (Format)
(Your Address)

Date: (Date)
To: (Tenant Name(s) & Address of the Property)
From: (Your Name & (Title)—Property Manager)
Subject: (Month, Year)—Drain Stoppage Fee
Account #: (Unit #/Year)

You are in violation of terms of the said rental agreement, which states, in part, "Water flow blockages are tenant's responsibility when caused by their own carelessness and/or negligence. Tenants will pay for any drain stoppages due to unnatural causes. This includes clogged toilets, clogged showers, clogged bathroom sinks and clogged kitchen sinks, and clogged washing machine outlets."

Further, "If the work is performed by the landlord's plumber or by a hired plumber, the property manager will provide tenants with a copy of the bill showing the work performed by the plumber in addition to $ (amount) management fees via U. S. mail."

Particulars of transactions

Invoice Number: XXX.............. $ (amount)
Management Fee..........................$ (amount)
Amount due..........................$ (amount)

Please Note: The above amount is due upon receipt.

If the above amount is not postmarked (self-addressed stamped envelope) on or before 2nd day of delivery of this notice,

(Your name)'s collection attorney will seek collection and may lead to eviction. Time is of the essence, and no excuses (ill health, job loss, financial emergency, etc.) will be accepted for late rent payment.

(Your name), Property Manager, Cell: XXX-XXX-XXXX (Emergency Only)

- -

Return This Portion With Your Payment. Thank You.
Please make check payable to: (Your Name)

TRANSACTION		TOTAL AMOUNT DUE
Tenant: (Name), (Complete address) Invoice Number: XXX.............. $ (amount) Management Fee..........................$ (amount) Amount due...............................**$ (amount)**		**$ (amount)**
Account #:(Unit #/Year)	**Billing Date: (Date)**	**Due Date: Due upon receipt**

Appendix B-7

No Rent + Per Day Penalty Letter (Format)
(Your Address)

Date: (Date)
To: (Tenant Name(s) & Address of the Property)
From: (Your Name & (Title)—Property Manager)
Subject: (Month, Year)—No Rent + per Day Penalty
Account #: (Unit #/Year)

You are in violation of terms of the said rental agreement, which states, in part, "Terms: resident agrees to pay in advance $ (amount) per month on the __1 st__ day of each month."

You are also in violation of the rent payment late charge of the said rental agreement, which states, in part, "A late fee of___$ (amount)__ , said amount not to exceed 6% of the monthly rent, shall be an additional payment if not received by the___5th__day of the month (post marked by 5th of the month).

You are also in violation of "rent payment late charge—beginning on 10th day: Rental payment received on or after the___10th__ of the month will incur additional per day penalty. A late fee of _$15.00 per day penalty_ will apply in addition to initial late fee of__$ (amount)_ (above). Attach a separate check of__$ (amount)__plus__$15.00 per day penalty__payable to _(your name)___ Any rent lost in the mail will be treated as unpaid until received by (your name)."

Particulars of transactions

Rent amount for the month of (Month), (Year)..........$ (amount)
Rent payment late charge..$ (amount)
Rent payment per day penalty beginning on the10th..$ (amount)

Total rent amount that was due for (Month), (Year)...$ (amount)

Please Note: The above amount is due upon receipt.

If the above amount is not postmarked (self-addressed stamped envelope) on or before 2nd day of delivery of this notice, (your name)'s collection attorney will seek collection and may lead to eviction. Time is of the essence, and no excuses (ill health, job loss, financial emergency, etc.) will be accepted for late rent payment.

(Your name), Property Manager, Cell: XXX-XXX-XXXX (Emergency Only)

- -

Return this portion with your payment. Thank you.
Please make check payable to: (Your Name)

TRANSACTION	TOTAL AMOUNT DUE
Tenant: (Name), (Complete address) Rent amount for the month of (Month), (Year).........$ (amount) Rent payment late charge...$ (amount) Rent payment per day penalty beginning on the10th..$ (amount) Total rent amount that was due for (Month), (Year)..**$ (amount)**	**$ (amount)**
Account #:(Unit #/Year) **Billing Date: (Date)**	**Due Date: Due upon receipt**

Appendix B-8

No Utilities Payment Letter (Format)
(Your Address)

Date: (Date)
To: (Tenant Name(s) & Address of the Property)
From: (Your Name & (Title)—Property Manager)
Subject: (Month, Year)—Utilities Unpaid
Account #: (Unit #/Year)

You are in violation of terms of the said rental agreement, which states, in part,

"Terms: resident agrees to pay utilities per month on the 30th day of each month."

Particulars of transactions

Utilities (Month), (Year).....................................$ (amount)
Total amount due (Month), (Year).....................$ (amount)

Please Note: The above amount is due upon receipt.

If the above amount is not postmarked (self-addressed stamped envelope) on or before 2nd day of delivery of this notice, (your name)'s collection attorney will seek collection and may lead to eviction. Time is of the essence, and no excuses (ill health, job loss, financial emergency, etc.) will be accepted for late rent payment.

(Your name), Property Manager, Cell: XXX-XXX-XXXX (Emergency Only)

- -

Return this portion with your payment. Thank you.
Please make check payable to: (Your Name)

TRANSACTION	**TOTAL AMOUNT DUE**
Tenant: (Name), (Complete address) Utilities (Month), (Year)...........................$ (amount) Total amount due (Month), (Year).............**$ (amount)**	**$ (amount)**
Account #:(Unit #/Year) **Billing Date: (Date)**	**Due Date: Due upon receipt**

Appendix B-9

Rent Check Bounce Letter (Format)
(Your Address)

Date: (Date)
To: (Tenant Name(s) & Address of the Property)
From: (Your Name & (Title)—Property Manager)
Subject: (Month, Year)—Your Rent Check Bounced
Account #: (Unit #/Year)

Check #: XXX, Check Dated: (date), Amount of Check: $ (amount)

Above check has bounced. (Your name)'s bank has returned the above check marked "Insufficient Funds." This is in violation of the rental agreement.

This is in violation of the rent check bounce policy of the said rental agreement, which states, in part, "A charge of ____$ (amount)____ or the amount charged by the bank shall be paid by the tenants for any check that is returned unpaid. Upon return or dishonor of any check tendered as payment of rent, late charges will be assessed as if no rental payment was attempted; therefore, rent payment late charge will apply."

This is also in violation of the rent payment late charge of the said rental agreement, which states, in part,

"A late fee of___$ (amount)___, said amount not to exceed 6% of the monthly rent, shall be an additional payment if not received by the___5th___day of the month (post marked by 5th of the month)."

Particulars of transactions

(Month, Year) rent check that bounced..........$ (amount)
Rent check bounce Fee....................................$ (amount)
Rent payment late charge.................................$ (amount)
Total amount due...$ (amount)

Please make cashier's check or money order payable to (your name), an amount of $ (amount).

Please Note: The above amount is due upon receipt.

If the above amount is not postmarked (self-addressed stamped envelope) on or before 2nd day of delivery of this notice, (your name)'s collection attorney will seek collection and may lead to eviction. Time is of the essence, and no excuses (ill health, job loss, financial emergency, etc.) will be accepted for late rent payment.

(Your name), Property Manager, Cell: XXX-XXX-XXXX (Emergency Only)

Return this portion with your payment. Thank you.
Please make check payable to: (Your Name)

TRANSACTION	**TOTAL AMOUNT DUE**
Tenant: (Name), (Complete address) (Month, Year) rent check that bounced.......$ (amount) Rent check bounce Fee..............................$ (amount) Rent Payment late charge............................$ (amount) Total amount due...**$ (amount)**	**$ (amount)**
Account #:(Unit #/Year) **Billing Date: (Date)**	**Due Date: Due upon receipt**

Appendix C

Appendix C-1

Paramount Property–Purchase Offer–Analysis Form

(Property Address)

Unit Mix

Unit #	Rms	Baths	Mo. Rent	Yr. Rent
1				
2				
3				
4				
Laundry				
Other				
Total PSORI				

Retirement Income & Expense Analysis

	Monthly	Yearly
TOTAL PSORI		
Less Vacancy		
Gross PSORI		
Less TOTAL OE		
NORI		
Less DS		
CF		

Operating Expenses

	Monthly	Yearly
Insurance		
Water		
Electric		
Gas		
Garbage		
Fire Inspection Fee		
County Health fee		
Environmental Fee		
Management		
Repairs and Maint.		
Property Tax		
Total OE		

CAP RATE	CASH ON CASH RETURN	DEBT COVERAGE RATIO
$CR = \frac{NORI_{(a)} \times 100}{V}$ $CR_{(\%)}$ desired = 6-12%	$CF = NORI_{(a)} - DS_{(a)}$ $COCR = \frac{CF \times 100}{AC}$ $COCR_{(\%)}$ desired = 10-20%	$DCR = \frac{NORI_{(a)}}{DS_{(a)}}$ DCR 0.50 = Negative CF DCR 1.00 = *Break Even* DCR 2.00 = Strong CF
Actual Calculations	Actual Calculations	Actual Calculations

GRM Calculations

$GRM = \frac{SP}{PSORI_{(a)}}$ GRM = (ONLY to compare with other similar listed properties for sale)	Actual Calculations

Appendix D

Appendix D-1

Prospective Tenant Card

Name	Cell #	# Bd/Ba	Max. Amt Requested
Date of Last Conversation: Reason for Wanting to Move in:			

Index

B

C

D

E

F

G

H

I

J

L

M

N

O

P

Q

R

T

V

W

Y

About the Author

Sam M. Ali has been a successful retirement investor for more than two decades and is a self-made millionaire and landlord who has used his own individual federal retirement fund—Thrift Savings Plan. His compelling reason for this doing so came from his peers at a federal government agency, the U. S. Food and Drug Administration (FDA), who suggested he write this book since he had already helped a number of them become retirement rich by using their own individual retirement funds. In fact, his passion for golden-years income stream became evident during the time when he became a landlord, not when he was a real-estate sales associate (1988-90). Over the years, he learned these skills slowly and perfected them (time-tested) while being a landlord. As a member of the Apartment Owners Association, he knows the ins and outs of real estate as a fitting path for retirement income. To protect his retirement assets, he has created two limited liability companies—Equity Advance Properties, LLC and California Housing Company, LLC. He is pleased to offer his insightful philosophy of building much-needed wealth for the golden years. Through his own experiences, he believes he has created local solutions to the retirement income dilemma facing middle-class Americans. As Sam says, the wisdom and strong advice of this book is truly a bridge over the troubled waters. He lives in South San Francisco, California, with his wife and daughter.

e|LIVE

---

listen|imagine|view|experience

AUDIO BOOK DOWNLOAD INCLUDED WITH THIS BOOK!

In your hands you hold a complete digital entertainment package. In addition to the paper version, you receive a free download of the audio version of this book. Simply use the code listed below when visiting our website. Once downloaded to your computer, you can listen to the book through your computer's speakers, burn it to an audio CD or save the file to your portable music device (such as Apple's popular iPod) and listen on the go!

How to get your free audio book digital download:

1. Visit www.tatepublishing.com and click on the e|LIVE logo on the home page.
2. Enter the following coupon code: fbfb-1ebf-e397-bb78-a461-c491-c917-ce1b
3. Download the audio book from your e|LIVE digital locker and begin enjoying your new digital entertainment package today!